AF421098

Table of Content

Unlock the Power of Derivatives

A Practical Guide to Trading Futures and Options in the Indian Market

APURVA PARIKH

Disclaimer

This book is intended for educational purposes only. All ideas, opinions, chart studies, and examples are presented solely for informational and educational use and should not be considered as trading or investment recommendations. The author disclaims any liability for financial loss, whether direct or indirect, resulting from the use of the material in this book. Investors and traders are encouraged to consult a qualified professional before making any trading or investment decisions.

While every effort has been made to verify the information within this book, neither the author nor the publisher assumes responsibility for any errors, omissions, or misuse of the content.

Dedication

This book is dedicated to all traders and investors who seek to master the art of derivatives trading. May it help you gain knowledge, build confidence, and achieve consistent success in the dynamic world of futures and options in India.

Acknowledgement

I am deeply grateful to my father, wife, son, and daughter for their constant support and belief in me. Your encouragement has been my biggest strength throughout this journey.

I have referred to the book ,*Equity Derivatives* from NISM and used platforms like TradingView and Opstra by Definedge AND Angelone for generating charts. These resources have been invaluable in shaping the content of this book.

I also extend my heartfelt thanks to my mentors. Their knowledge and guidance have helped me simplify this complex topic and present it in a way that is easy to understand.

Preface

Derivatives trading has long been perceived as complex and risky, often leaving many traders and investors hesitant to explore its true potential. However, when understood and applied correctly, derivatives can be powerful tools for risk management, speculation, and wealth creation. **This book, *Unlock the Power of Derivatives*, is designed to simplify the concepts of futures and options trading in the Indian stock market** and make them accessible to traders at all levels.

Through years of experience in the financial markets, I have seen traders struggle due to a lack of structured knowledge. Many rely on tips and market rumors rather than a solid understanding of derivatives. **My goal with this book is to bridge that gap by providing clear, practical insights that traders can use to make informed decisions.**

The book follows a step-by-step approach, starting from the fundamentals of derivatives and gradually moving towards advanced trading strategies. It covers key aspects like futures and options pricing, risk management, and real-world application using tools and platforms widely used in India. More importantly, **it emphasizes practical learning, ensuring that**

readers can apply these concepts confidently in live markets.

Whether you are a beginner looking to understand the basics or an experienced trader aiming to refine your strategies, this book will serve as a valuable guide in your trading journey. I invite you to explore the exciting world of derivatives and unlock its potential for financial growth.

About the author

Mr. Apurva Parikh is a TEDx speaker, bestselling author, and renowned finance coach with 18 years of experience in the financial world. As a Visiting Faculty at Ahmedabad Management Association (AMA) and BSE Institute, he mentors traders, investors, and fintech startups.

An NISM-Certified Research Analyst with multiple NSE certifications, he has authored 10 bestselling books, simplifying finance for millions. With a passion for financial literacy, he continues to inspire and empower individuals toward wealth creation and trading success.

Books by Author

https://www.amazon.in/Secrets-Financial-Freedom-Women-Protect-ebook/dp/B08JQQGRG5

https://www.amazon.in/Financial-Secrets-Entrepreneurs-Insiders-Enterprises-ebook/dp/B08NHN9WDN

https://www.amazon.in/Secrets-Improve-Your-CIBIL-Score-ebook/dp/B08YVQKT47

https://www.amazon.in/Financial-Mistakes-that-keep-poor-ebook/dp/B093FHKSFC

https://www.amazon.in/Secrets-find-Value-Stocks-Consistently-ebook/dp/B0BMLL4Q6Z

https://www.amazon.in/51-Money-Rules-Financial-Strategies-ebook/dp/B0DH38JGTY

https://www.amazon.in/Traders-Mindset-Psychology-Discipline-Long-Term-ebook/dp/B0DKNZW712/

https://www.amazon.in/Profile-Simplified-Mastering-Movements-simplified-ebook/dp/B0DLV2WH51

https://www.amazon.in/Colour-Candles-Revolutionize-Integrated-Candlestick-ebook/dp/B0DRCG88N4

If you want to learn Stock Market from him, you may contact him at contact@financewithapurva.com or whatsapp @ 919879184987

Words from Authors

Trading derivatives is like playing a game of chess—strategy, patience, and risk management decide whether you win or lose. Yet, many traders enter the market without understanding the rules, only to face losses and frustration. I have seen this happen countless times. That is why I wrote this book—to simplify the complex world of futures and options and help traders make informed decisions instead of emotional ones.

Over the years, I have coached thousands of traders and investors. One thing I have realized is that most people fear derivatives because they seem complicated. But the truth is, once you understand the basics and apply the right strategies, derivatives can become a powerful tool for managing risk and increasing profits. This book is my attempt to make learning derivatives easy and practical for every trader, whether beginner or experienced.

I have structured this book in a way that guides you step by step—from understanding how derivatives work to using advanced trading strategies. You will find real-life examples, case studies, and practical insights that will help you apply what you learn in actual trading scenarios. I have also included valuable tools and platforms that traders in India use daily, making this book a complete guide for mastering derivatives trading.

My goal is simple: by the time you finish this book, you should feel confident in trading futures and options. You should be able to plan your trades wisely, control your risks, and avoid common mistakes that trap most traders.

The journey to becoming a successful derivatives trader starts with knowledge. So, let's begin this journey together and unlock the true power of derivatives!

Apurva Parikh

Chapter 1: The Foundation of Derivatives

Arun is a 27-year-old IT professional who invests and trades in the stock market. However, he lacks a proper understanding of derivatives but wants to trade practically without learning the theory. Seeking guidance, he approaches his friend Ravi, a Certified Research Analyst and an experienced options trader, to learn about derivatives.

Arun: I want to buy 1 lot of Nifty options. Can you teach me how to buy?

Ravi: How much are you looking to invest?

Arun: ₹5,000. I want to learn.

Ravi: Alright, but shall we first go over some theory on what derivatives are and how they work?

Arun: Please show me practically how to buy first, then explain the theory.

Ravi: Okay

Right now, Nifty is trading at ₹22,902. Today's date is March 19, 2025.

Let's purchase a Nifty Call Option—1 lot with a strike price of ₹23,000, expiring on March 20, 2025. I will show you the process through my broker account.

Here, the price is ₹43.45. So, the total investment required is ₹3,367, as shown here. If you have the required balance, place a buy order, and your order will be executed.

Arun: Can you please explain what information I need to search for when buying an option?

Ravi: You need to look for:

1. The option you want to buy (in this case, Nifty 23,000 Call Option).
2. The expiry date (here, March 20, 2025)

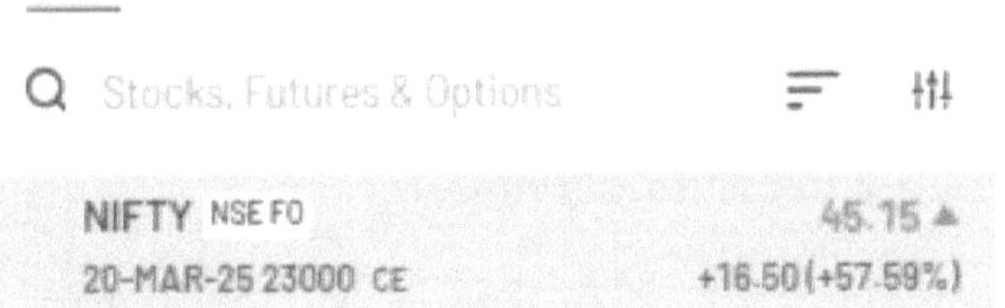

Arun: Thanks a lot! Now, please explain the theory part.

Ravi: Okay.

1.1 Demystifying Derivatives: The Basics

Derivatives in the stock market are financial instruments that derive their value from an underlying asset, such as stocks, commodities, currencies, or indices. Unlike direct ownership of stocks, derivatives are contracts between parties with specific terms and conditions.

The most common types of stock market derivatives include:

Options: Contracts giving the buyer the right (but not obligation) to buy (call option) or sell (put option) an underlying asset at a predetermined price before a specific date. Options are used for hedging risk or speculating on price movements.

Futures: Agreements to buy or sell an asset at a fixed price on a future date. Unlike options, futures represent an obligation to complete the transaction. Stock index futures like the S&P 500 E-mini are popular among institutional investors.

Swaps: Contracts where parties exchange cash flows or liabilities. Equity swaps allow investors to exchange returns from a stock or index for another investment's returns.

Forwards: Similar to futures but customized and traded over-the-counter rather than on exchanges.

Derivatives serve several important functions:

- Risk management (hedging against adverse price movements)
- Price discovery (helping determine fair market values)
- Market efficiency (allowing for arbitrage opportunities)
- Leverage (controlling larger positions with smaller capital)

However, derivatives also come with risks, including counterparty risk, leverage risk, and market risk. The 2008 financial crisis highlighted how complex derivatives like credit default swaps can amplify systemic risks when misused.

For individual investors, understanding derivatives is crucial for portfolio protection and potentially enhancing returns, though they require careful study before implementation.

1.2 Evolution of the Global & Indian Derivatives Market

Derivatives have a very old history dating back many centuries. They didn't start in modern stock markets but came from simple business needs long ago.

In the 12th Century, European traders at market fairs began making contracts for future delivery of goods. This helped both buyers and sellers plan ahead. By the 13th Century, English monasteries were selling their wool up to 20 years in advance to foreign merchants, showing early forms of futures contracts.

One famous early derivatives story is the "Tulip Mania" in Holland (1634-1637). People got extremely excited about tulip bulbs and started trading futures contracts for them. Prices went very high before suddenly crashing, causing many people to lose their money.

In Japan in the late 17th Century, a rice futures market developed near Osaka. This helped rice farmers protect themselves from problems like bad weather or wars that could destroy their crops.

The modern derivatives market really took shape in America. In 1848, the Chicago Board of Trade (CBOT) started allowing trading of forward contracts on farm products. By 1865, they created the first proper "exchange traded" futures contracts.

Other important steps happened when:

- The Chicago Mercantile Exchange (CME) formed in 1919
- Currency futures started trading in 1972
- The first options exchange opened in 1973
- Interest rate futures began in 1975
- Stock index futures launched in 1982

These developments helped businesses manage risks better. Farmers could lock in prices for their crops before harvest. Companies could protect themselves from changes in currency values or interest rates.

Today's derivatives market includes many products like futures, options, and swaps. While these financial tools can be complicated, they started from the simple human need to create certainty in an uncertain world and protect against future price changes.

1.3 Inside the Indian Derivatives Market

The Indian derivatives market is quite young compared to global markets, starting officially only in the early 2000s. Let me explain how it all began.

In 1996, SEBI (Securities and Exchange Board of India) took the first step by forming a committee led by Dr. L.C. Gupta. This committee submitted its report in March 1998, suggesting that derivatives should be treated as 'securities' so they could be regulated under existing rules. Soon after, Professor J.R. Varma led another group to recommend safety measures for the derivatives market, covering important aspects like margin requirements and monitoring systems.

A major breakthrough happened in 1999 when the government changed the Securities Contract Regulation Act to include derivatives as securities. Then in March 2000, the government removed an old rule that had banned forward trading for three decades.

Exchange-traded derivatives finally began in India in June 2000 when SEBI allowed BSE and NSE to start derivatives trading. The first products were index futures based on Nifty and Sensex. After this initial step, the market expanded step by step:

- Index options started in June 2001
- Options on individual stocks began in July 2001
- Futures on individual stocks were introduced in November 2001

Later, in February 2013, the Metropolitan Stock Exchange of India (MSEI) also joined the derivatives market.

Over the years, the Indian derivatives market has grown significantly. Today, NSE has become one of the world's largest derivatives exchanges, especially for index options. The market has helped many investors and businesses manage their financial risks better. SEBI continues to update regulations to ensure the market remains safe while supporting economic growth.

1.4 Types of Derivatives

Derivatives are classified into four main categories:

Derivatives are financial tools whose value comes from another asset (called the underlying asset). There are four main types of derivatives used in India and worldwide. Let me explain each one in simple terms:

1. Forwards

Forward contracts are private agreements between two parties to buy or sell something at a fixed price on a future date. These are not traded on stock exchanges but directly between parties (Over-The-Counter or OTC).

For example, a wheat farmer worried about falling prices might make a forward contract with a flour mill to sell 1000 kg of wheat at Rs. 25/kg three months later. This protects both parties - the farmer knows exactly how much money he'll get, and the mill knows exactly how much it will pay, regardless of market price changes.

2. Futures

Futures contracts are similar to forwards but are standardized and traded on exchanges like NSE or

BSE. They have fixed lot sizes, expiry dates, and other terms set by the exchange.

For example, if you expect the Nifty 50 index to rise, you can buy a Nifty futures contract. If Nifty goes up as expected, you make a profit; if it falls, you face a loss. The advantage of futures over forwards is that they are more liquid and have less counterparty risk.

3. Options

Options give the buyer the right (but not the obligation) to buy or sell something at a specific price within a certain time period. The buyer pays a small amount called premium for this right.

There are two types:

- Call Options: Right to buy at a specified price
- Put Options: Right to sell at a specified price

For example, if you buy a Reliance Industries call option with a strike price of Rs. 2800, and the stock rises to Rs. 3000, you can exercise your option to buy at Rs. 2800 and profit from the difference.

4. Swaps

Swaps are agreements to exchange cash flows based on different variables. They're commonly used by companies to manage various risks.

For instance, a company expecting to receive US dollars might use a currency swap to protect itself from unfavorable exchange rate changes. Similarly, interest rate swaps help companies manage interest rate risks on their loans.

These derivative instruments help investors and businesses manage financial risks and sometimes generate profits through speculative trading. However, derivatives can be complex and involve significant risks, so proper knowledge is essential before trading them

1.5 Who's Who in the Derivatives World? (Market Participants)

The derivatives market has three key participants:

1. **Hedgers:** They use derivatives to protect themselves from price fluctuations. For example, a farmer may sell wheat futures to lock in a selling price.

2. **Speculators:** They trade derivatives to profit from market movements. Traders often use derivatives because they provide leverage, allowing them to control larger positions with less capital.

3. **Arbitrageurs:** They exploit price differences between two markets to make risk-free profits. For instance, if Gold is trading at Rs. 60,000 in Delhi and Rs. 60,200 in Mumbai, an arbitrageur can buy low in Delhi and sell high in Mumbai.

1.6 The Two Faces of Derivatives: Exchange-Traded vs. OTC Markets

Derivatives can be traded in two ways:

1. Exchange-Traded Derivatives (ETD): These are standardized contracts traded on recognized exchanges such as **NSE** or **BSE**. They are regulated and have low counterparty risk due to a clearing corporation that guarantees settlement.

2. Over-the-Counter (OTC) Derivatives: These are customized contracts traded directly between parties. While they offer flexibility, they carry higher counterparty risk.

1.7 Why Derivatives Matter: Their Role in Modern Finance

Derivatives play a crucial role in financial markets:

Risk Management: Derivatives allow participants to hedge against price volatility.

Price Discovery: Futures and options markets provide valuable insights into expected asset prices.

Liquidity Enhancement: Derivatives enhance market liquidity, ensuring smoother transactions.

Portfolio Diversification: Investors can use derivatives to access multiple asset classes and manage risk efficiently.

1.8 Risk Factors in Derivatives Trading: What Every Trader Must Know

While derivatives offer significant opportunities, they also involve risks such as:

Market Risk: Losses due to adverse price movements.

Credit Risk: Risk of counterparty default.

Liquidity Risk: Difficulty in exiting positions in low-volume markets.

Operational Risk: Errors in trade execution, fraud, or system failures.

Legal Risk: Regulatory uncertainties or unenforceable contracts.

Conclusion

Derivatives are powerful financial instruments that help traders and investors manage risk, speculate on price movements, and improve market efficiency. Over time, the Indian derivatives market has grown significantly, offering various products like futures and options. However, while derivatives provide many opportunities, they also carry risks that every trader must understand. By learning the basics, knowing the market participants, and recognizing the difference

between exchange-traded and OTC markets, one can
build a strong foundation for successful derivatives
trading.

Chapter 2: Stock Market Indices – The Pulse of the Market

Arun: I have a total equity portfolio of Rs. 50 lakhs. I fear that if the market falls, my entire portfolio will suffer. Can you suggest what I should do in this situation? I don't want to profit from the decline; I just want to protect my portfolio.

Ravi: You can use derivatives for hedging.

Arun: Please explain what I should do. I want to hedge my portfolio as I believe the market will fall, but I don't want to sell my holdings.

Ravi: The first step is to hedge your portfolio with index futures.

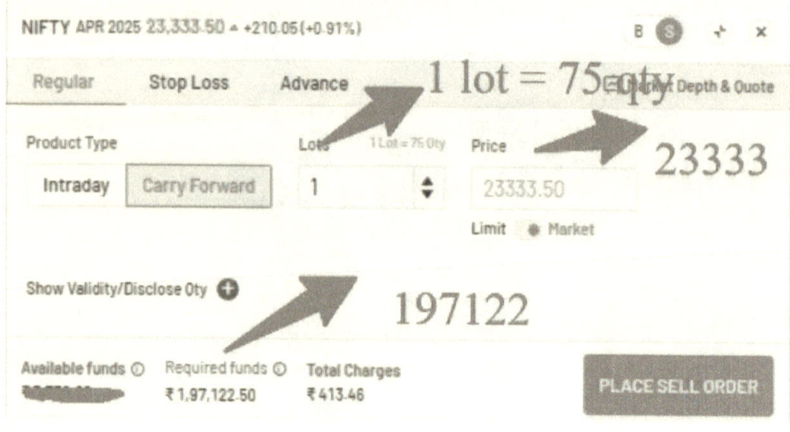

To hedge your portfolio, you need to take a short position (sell futures). One lot of Nifty consists of 75 units.

Step 1: Calculating the Initial Hedge

The current Nifty price is **23,333**, so the value of **one lot** is:

$$23,333 \times 75 = 17,50,000 \text{ (approx.)}$$

Since your total portfolio value is **Rs. 50 lakhs**, you need to determine how many lots are required to hedge the full amount:

$$50,00,000 \backslash 17,50,000 = 3 \text{ lots (approximately)}$$

Period	Long Term Beta *
RELIANCE Beta	1.23
Mean	1270.45
Standard Deviation	6.56
RELIANCE Beta	1.23

Period	Long Term Beta *
TCS Beta	0.910
Mean	3593.24
Standard Deviation	5.78
TCS Beta	0.910

Step 2: Adjusting for Portfolio Beta

Next, you need to calculate the **beta** of your portfolio. Beta measures the volatility of your portfolio relative to the benchmark index (Nifty).

To find this, take the **weighted average beta** of all the stocks in your portfolio. For example, if the calculated weighted average beta of your portfolio is **1.3**, then the effective value that needs to be hedged is:

$$50,00,000 \times 1.3 = 65,00,000$$

Now, to hedge this adjusted portfolio value, the number of Nifty futures lots required is:

$$65,00,000 \backslash 17,50,000 = 4 \text{ lots}$$

Step 3: Margin Requirement

To sell **4 lots of Nifty futures**, you need to maintain a margin. If the margin required per lot is **Rs. 1.97 lakhs**, then for 4 lots, the total margin required is:

$$1.97 \times 4 = 7.88 \text{ lakhs}$$

Outcome of the Hedge

- **If the market falls**, your portfolio value will decline, but you will recover the losses through profits from selling Nifty futures.
- **If the market rises**, you will incur a loss on the short Nifty futures position, but this loss will be offset by the increase in the value of your portfolio.

This strategy ensures that your portfolio is protected from market downturns while allowing you to retain your equity investments.

In this way, you can hedge your portfolio even market move up or down.

Arun- Thanks a lot Ravi, now please proceed towards theory part.

Ravi - okay

Think of the stock market as a giant cricket match. Each company is a player, and their share price is how many runs they've scored. But how do you quickly tell how the whole team (the market) is doing? That's what a stock index does. It's like the overall scoreboard for a particular part of the market.

2.1 Understanding Stock Indices: The Market's Scoreboard

A stock index is a selected group of stocks that represent a specific market segment or the overall market. The selection isn't random; it's carefully chosen based on certain rules.

For example:

NIFTY 50: This is the "Top 50 Companies" list on the NSE (National Stock Exchange). It shows how the biggest and most important companies in India are performing.

NIFTY Bank: This only looks at banks. It tells you how the banking sector is doing.

The index value changes based on the prices of the stocks in it. If most companies in the NIFTY 50 are seeing their share prices rise, the NIFTY 50 index goes up. If they're mostly falling, the index goes down.

In simple terms: A stock index is like a summary of how a particular section of the stock market is performing.

2.2 Why Indices Matter: A Trader's Guide to Market Trends

Stock indices are more than just numbers. They're helpful for many reasons:

Measuring Performance (Like a Benchmark): Imagine you've invested in a mutual fund. How do you know if it's doing well? You compare its returns to an index like the NIFTY 50. If your fund is growing faster than the NIFTY 50, your fund manager is likely doing a good job.

Market Sentiment (Mood of the Market): A rising index usually means investors are optimistic and buying stocks (bullish market). A falling index suggests they're worried and selling stocks (bearish market).

Derivatives: Indices are used as the basis for futures and options contracts. People can trade these contracts to bet on whether an index will go up or down.

Economic Health: A strong stock market (rising indices) often signals a healthy economy. A weak market can indicate economic problems.

Passive Investing: You can invest in "index funds" or "ETFs" that are designed to track an index like the NIFTY 50. This is an easy way to invest in a broad range of stocks at once.

2.3 Different Types of Stock Indices & Their Significance

Like different kinds of shops, there are different kinds of indices:

Broad Market Indices: These show the overall performance of the entire stock market. Examples are the NIFTY 50 and the SENSEX.

Sector Indices: These track specific sectors, like the NIFTY Bank (banks), NIFTY IT (IT companies), or NIFTY Pharma (pharmaceutical companies).

Size-Based Indices: These categorize companies by their market capitalization (total value of their shares). You'll see large-cap (big companies), mid-cap (medium companies), and small-cap (small companies) indices.

Strategy Indices: These Indices are based on specific investment strategies like dividend yield, value or growth.

2.4 Key Features That Define an Index

A good index should have these characteristics:

Representative: It should accurately reflect the market or sector it's supposed to track.

Objective: The selection process and rules should be fair and transparent.

Measurable: It should be easy to calculate and understand.

Replicable: It should be possible to create an investment portfolio that closely matches the index's performance.

Transparent: The rules for selecting stocks, how the index is calculated, and when it's rebalanced should be public knowledge.

2.5 How Indices Are Managed & Rebalanced

Indices aren't static; they need to be managed to stay relevant:

Periodic Reviews: Regularly checking if the companies in the index still accurately represent the market.

Rebalancing: Adjusting the weights of the companies to maintain the desired weighting scheme (e.g., based on market capitalization).

Constituent Changes: Adding or removing companies from the index based on mergers, acquisitions, or changes in their market capitalization.

2.6 Major Stock Indices in India & Their Impact

NIFTY 50: The flagship index of the National Stock Exchange (NSE), representing the top 50 companies.

SENSEX: The benchmark index of the Bombay Stock Exchange (BSE), comprising the 30 largest and most actively traded stocks.

NIFTY Bank: Tracks the performance of the banking sector.

NIFTY IT: Focuses on the information technology sector.

2.7 Practical Uses of Indices for Traders & Investors

Here are some ways you can use your understanding of indices:

Investment Decisions: Identify promising sectors for investment.

Portfolio Diversification: Use index funds or ETFs to get broad market exposure.

Risk Management: Use index futures and options to protect your portfolio from market downturns.

Performance Evaluation: Compare your investment performance to relevant indices.

Market Analysis: Monitor index movements to understand market sentiment and identify trends.

Stock indices are essential tools for understanding the stock market and making informed investment decisions. By understanding how indices work, you can become a more successful investor.

Conclusion

Stock market indices act like a mirror, reflecting the overall market's health and trends. They help traders and investors make informed decisions by tracking market movements and identifying opportunities. Understanding different types of indices, their features, and how they are managed is crucial for anyone in the stock market. In India, major indices like the Nifty and Sensex play a key role. By using indices wisely, traders and investors can navigate the market with better confidence and strategy.

Chapter 3: Forwards & Futures – The Building Blocks of Derivatives

Arun: Is it possible to earn from futures regardless of whether the market moves up or down?

Ravi: Yes, you can use an arbitrage strategy.

Arun: How does it work?

Ravi: Let me explain with a scenario.

Illustration: Cash-and-Carry Arbitrage

Let's consider stock **A** with the following details:

- **Cash market price**: Rs. 1,500
- **3-month futures price**: Rs. 1,550
- **Contract size**: 100 shares per futures contract
- **Cost of carry**: 9% per annum (approximately 0.75% per month)

Step 1: Calculating the Theoretical Price of the Futures Contract

The fair price of the 3-month futures contract is calculated using the formula:

$$\text{Fair Price} = \text{Spot Price} \times e^{\text{cost of carry} \times \text{time in months}}$$

$$= 1500 \times e^{0.0075 \times 3}$$

$$= 1500 \times e^{0.09 \times 3/12}$$

$$= 1534.13$$

Since the actual futures price (Rs. 1,550) is higher than the theoretical price (Rs. 1,534.13), the futures contract is overvalued.

Step 2: Executing the Arbitrage Strategy

To take advantage of this mispricing, an arbitrageur can:

1. **Buy 100 shares** of stock **A** in the cash market at **Rs. 1,500 per share.**
2. **Sell 1 futures contract** at **Rs. 1,550.**

This results in an **arbitrage profit** of:

$(1550-1534.13) \times 100 = 1587 (1550 - 1534.13) \times 100 = 1587 (1550-1534.13) \times 100 = 1587$

Step 3: Evaluating Different Market Scenarios at Expiry

Case I: Stock Price Rises to Rs. 1,580 at Expiry

- **Profit on the underlying stock:**

$(1580-1500) \times 100 = 8{,}000 (1580 - 1500) \times 100 = 8{,}000 (1580-1500) \times 100 = 8{,}000$

- **Loss on the futures contract:**

$(1580-1550)\times100=3,000(1580 - 1550) \times 100 = 3,000(1580-1550)\times100=3,000$

- **Total gain from arbitrage:**

$8,000-3,000=5,000,8,000 - 3,000 = 5,000,8,000-3,000=5,000$

- **Cost of financing (Cost of Carry):**

$34.13\times100=3,41334.13 \times 100 = 3,41334.13\times100=3,413$

- **Net arbitrage profit:**

$5,000-3,413=1,5875,000 - 3,413 = 1,5875,000-3,413=1,587$

Case II: Stock Price Falls to Rs. 1,480 at Expiry

- **Loss on the underlying stock:**

$(1500-1480)\times100=2,000(1500 - 1480) \times 100 = 2,000(1500-1480)\times100=2,000$

- **Profit on the futures contract:**

$(1550-1480)\times100=7,000(1550 - 1480) \times 100 = 7,000(1550-1480)\times100=7,000$

- **Total gain from arbitrage:**

7,000−2,000=5,0007,000 - 2,000 = 5,0007,000−2,000=5,000

- **Cost of financing (Cost of Carry):**

34.13×100=3,41334.13 \times 100 = 3,41334.13×100=3,413

- **Net arbitrage profit:**

5,000−3,413=1,5875,000 - 3,413 = 1,5875,000−3,413=1,587

Conclusion

Regardless of whether the stock price rises or falls, the arbitrageur locks in a **risk-free profit of Rs. 1,587**. This strategy works because the mispricing between the actual and theoretical futures price provides an opportunity to earn a profit with minimal risk.

Arun- Thanks a lot, now lets move back to theory part.

Ravi- Okay

Imagine you're a farmer growing wheat. You're worried about the price of wheat fluctuating by the time you harvest. Or, imagine you're a biscuit factory owner. You want to lock in a price for wheat now so you can plan your costs. This is where forwards and futures come in – they're tools that allow you to agree on a price for something *today*, for delivery *later*. This chapter breaks down these powerful but often misunderstood concepts.

3.1 Forward Contracts: The First Type of Derivative

A **forward contract** is an agreement between two parties to buy or sell an asset at a fixed price on a future date. This is one of the earliest forms of derivatives because its value depends on the price of an underlying asset.

Unlike contracts traded on exchanges, **forward contracts are customized** and traded **privately** (Over-the-Counter or OTC). This allows both parties to set the terms as per their needs.

Example of a Forward Contract

Let's say a farmer grows wheat and is worried that prices may fall before his harvest. To secure a fair price, he makes a forward contract with a local buyer.

- They agree that the farmer will sell **100 quintals of wheat at ₹2,000 per quintal** after three months.
- If, at the time of harvest, the market price **falls to ₹1,800 per quintal**, the farmer still sells at **₹2,000 per quintal**, avoiding a loss.
- If the market price **rises to ₹2,200 per quintal**, the buyer benefits because he gets wheat at a cheaper rate.

Thus, forward contracts help both buyers and sellers reduce their risk due to price changes in the market.

3.2 Futures Contracts: A More Systematic Approach

A **futures contract** is a standardized agreement to buy or sell an asset at a fixed price on a specific future date.

Unlike forward contracts, **futures are traded on exchanges**, making them more organized, secure, and transparent.

Example of a Futures Contract

Imagine a rice mill owner who needs **1,000 quintals of rice** for processing after three months. He fears prices might go up and wants to fix a purchase price.

- He enters into a **futures contract** with a seller at **₹1,500 per quintal**.
- If, at the time of delivery, the price **rises to ₹1,700 per quintal**, he still pays **only ₹1,500 per quintal**, saving money.
- If the price **falls to ₹1,400 per quintal**, he still has to buy at ₹1,500, paying more than the market price.

Futures contracts help businesses and traders protect themselves from sudden price changes, ensuring stable costs.

3.3 Understanding Futures Contracts: Key Features

A **futures contract** is similar to a forward contract, but there is one big difference—it is **standardized and traded on an exchange**. The exchange decides the terms of the contract, including:

- The **quantity and quality** of the asset
- The **delivery dates**
- The **trading rules**

This standardization makes futures contracts more **liquid** (easier to buy and sell) and **reduces default risk**.

Example of a Futures Contract

An investor believes that the **NIFTY 50 index** will go **up** next month. So, he **buys a NIFTY 50 futures contract** at a set price.

- If the **NIFTY 50 rises above this price on expiry,** he makes a profit.
- If the **NIFTY 50 falls below this price**, he incurs a loss.

Key Characteristics of Futures Contracts

- **Standardized:** The exchange sets the contract terms.

- **Exchange-Traded:** These contracts are bought and sold on a recognized exchange.
- **Marked-to-Market:** Profits and losses are settled daily.
- **Lower Risk:** A clearinghouse guarantees the contract, reducing the chance of default.

3.4 Contract Specifications: Understanding the Details

Every futures contract has specific terms that define the agreement. The important details include:

☑ **Contract Size:** The amount of the asset covered in one contract (e.g., 50 shares of a stock, a certain weight of gold).

☑ **Tick Size:** The smallest price change allowed (e.g., ₹0.05).

☑ **Delivery Date:** The date when the asset must be delivered.

☑ **Expiry Date:** The last day the contract can be traded.

☑ **Underlying Asset:** The asset linked to the contract (e.g., a stock, an index).

Practical Example: NIFTY 50 Futures Contract

Let's say you are looking at a **NIFTY 50 futures contract**. The specifications might be:

- **Contract Size:** 50 (each point movement in NIFTY 50 equals ₹50)
- **Tick Size:** 0.05
- **Expiry Date:** Last Thursday of the month

This means that if you buy **one NIFTY 50 futures contract**, you are basically betting on **50 times the NIFTY 50 index value** in the future.

Futures contracts are widely used by traders and investors to **manage risk and take advantage of price movements in financial markets**.

3.5 Important Terms Every Futures Trader Should Know

To trade futures successfully, you must understand some key terms:

◆ **Long Position:** Buying a futures contract because you expect the price to **go up**.

◆ **Short Position:** Selling a futures contract because you expect the price to **go down**.

◆ **Margin:** The initial deposit you must pay to enter a futures trade. This is **not** the full contract value but a small percentage to cover possible losses.

◆ **Mark-to-Market (MTM):** The daily process of adjusting your profit or loss in your account based on the current market price of the futures contract.

◆ **Expiry:** The last date when a futures contract can be traded.

◆ **Settlement:** The process of completing the contract on expiry. This can be done in two ways:

- **Physical Delivery:** The actual asset (e.g., gold, wheat) is delivered.
- **Cash Settlement:** The price difference is paid instead of delivering the asset.

Understanding these terms will help you trade futures with confidence! 🚀

3.6 Forwards vs. Futures: Key Differences Explained

Feature	Forward Contract	Futures Contract
Standardization	Customized	Standardized
Trading Venue	Over-the-Counter (OTC)	Exchange-Traded
Credit Risk	Higher (Default Risk)	Lower (Clearinghouse)
Liquidity	Lower	Higher
Regulation	Less Regulated	Highly Regulated
Mark-to-Market	Typically No	Yes

3.7 Who Uses Futures? (And Why?)

Futures contracts are used by different types of market participants, each with their own reasons:

◆ **Hedgers:** These are companies or individuals who want to protect themselves from price changes.

- Example: A **jeweller** buys gold futures to lock in a price, avoiding the risk of gold becoming more expensive.
- A **farmer** sells wheat futures to secure a fixed price before harvest, protecting against a price drop.

◆ **Speculators:** These are traders who take risks to **earn profits** from price movements.

- Example: An **investor** buys a NIFTY 50 futures contract, hoping the index will rise and he can sell at a profit.

◆ **Arbitrageurs:** These traders make **risk-free profits** by buying in one market and selling in another at a higher price.

- Example: If gold is cheaper in one market and costlier in another, an arbitrageur buys in the cheaper market and sells in the costlier one to earn a guaranteed profit.

3.8 Example: Hedging with Futures

A **software company** expects a big payment in **US dollars** in three months. They are worried that the

rupee may strengthen against the dollar. If this happens, their dollar payment will be worth fewer rupees when converted.

☑ To **hedge** this risk, they sell **dollar futures contracts**, locking in today's exchange rate. ☑ When the payment arrives, even if the rupee has strengthened, the company still gets the same value in rupees.

This is how businesses use futures to **protect themselves from currency fluctuations**.

3.9 The Power of Futures: Managing Risk and Seizing Opportunities

Futures contracts are **powerful financial tools** that help traders and businesses:

✔ **Manage risk** (Hedging)
✔ **Profit from price movements** (Speculation)
✔ **Take advantage of price differences** (Arbitrage)

Understanding **how forwards and futures work** is essential for anyone involved in financial markets. With the right knowledge of **futures trading strategies, market terms, and contract mechanisms**, you can trade with confidence!

3.10 Payoff Charts for Futures Contracts

What is a Payoff Chart?

A **payoff chart** is a simple way to **see profits and losses** from a financial trade. It shows how much money you can make (or lose) based on how the **price of an asset** (like stocks, gold, or oil) changes when the contract expires.

📌 **X-axis (Horizontal Line):** Shows the **price of the asset** at expiry.
📌 **Y-axis (Vertical Line):** Shows **profit or loss**.

- **If the line goes up** → Profit
- **If the line goes down** → Loss

Payoff Charts for Futures (Simple Explanation)

☑ **Long Position (Buyer's Payoff)**

- If the asset **price goes up**, the buyer makes **unlimited profit** (they can buy at a lower agreed price and sell at a higher market price).
- If the **price falls**, the buyer faces **unlimited loss** (they must buy at the agreed higher price, even if the market price is lower).

- If the **price rises**, the seller faces **unlimited loss** (they must sell at the agreed lower price, even if the market price is higher).

Understanding payoff charts helps traders plan their positions and manage their risk effectively in futures trading!

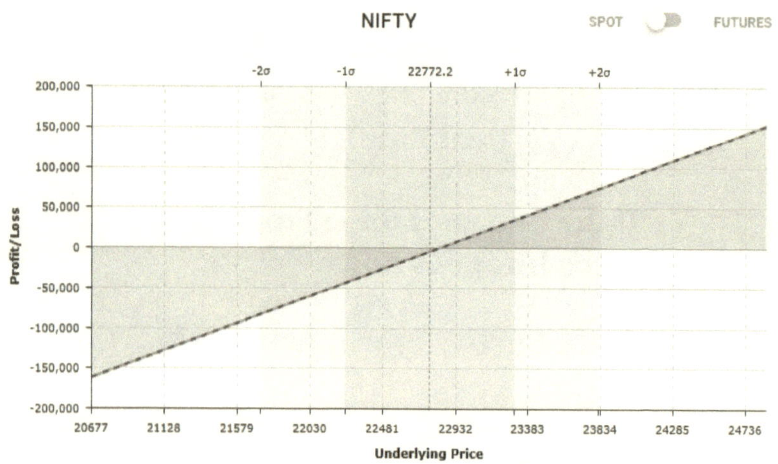

Short Position (Seller's Payoff)

- If the **price falls**, the seller makes **unlimited profit** (they can sell at the higher agreed price and buy back at a lower market price).
- If the **price rises**, the seller faces **unlimited loss** (they must sell at the agreed lower price, even if the market price is higher).

Understanding payoff charts helps traders plan their positions and manage their risk effectively in futures trading! 🚀

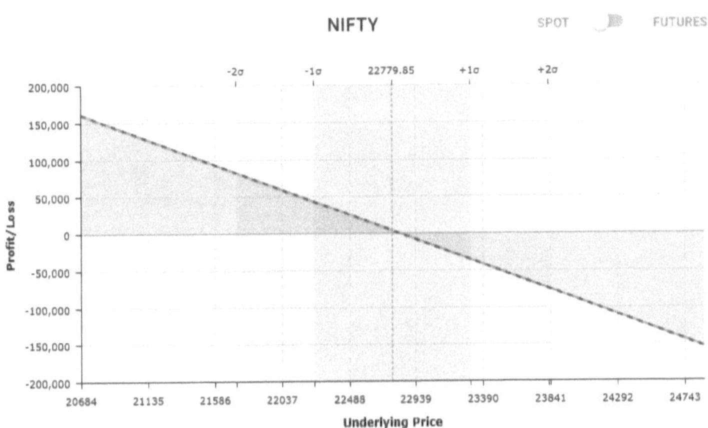

Conclusion

Forwards and futures are essential tools in the world of derivatives, helping traders, investors, and businesses manage risk and take advantage of market opportunities. While forwards are private agreements, futures are standardized contracts traded on exchanges, making them more secure and accessible. Understanding key features, contract specifications, and important terms is crucial for every trader. By learning how futures can be used for hedging and speculation, one can make informed decisions. Payoff charts further help in visualizing potential profits and losses. Mastering these basics lays a strong foundation for success in the derivatives market.

Chapter 4: Options Trading – Unlocking the Power of Flexibility

Arun: Is it possible to profit if I fear the market will decline while keeping my losses limited?

Ravi: Yes, you can buy **put options**. By doing so, you only need to pay a **premium**, which is your **maximum loss**. However, if the market falls significantly, your **potential profit can be substantial**.

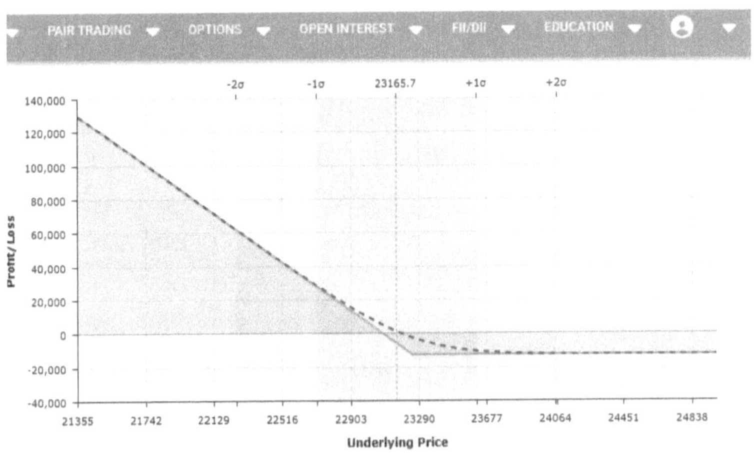

For example, if you buy a **put option** with a **strike price of 23,250** expiring on **March 27, 2025**, you will need to pay a **premium of Rs. 12,600**. This **premium amount is your maximum possible loss**. However, if the market falls significantly, the value of your put option will increase, allowing you to earn a substantial profit. Let me explain practically

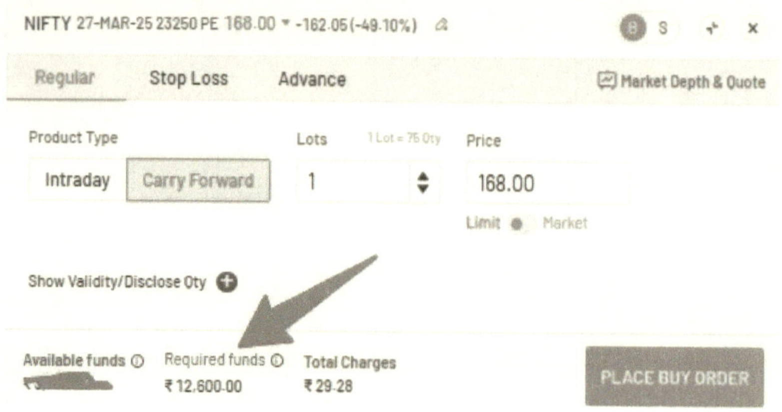

Arun- Thanks Ravi

Ravi- Now lets move on

Imagine you're at a car auction. Instead of bidding to *buy* a car outright, you bid for the *option* to buy a car at a specific price within a set time. If you win the option and the car's value goes up, you can buy it and make a profit. If the car's value goes down, you simply let the option expire, losing only the small amount you paid for the option itself. This is the basic idea behind options, a powerful tool for both managing risk and seeking profit in the stock market.

4.1 The Essentials of Options Trading

Unlike futures, which *obligate* you to buy or sell an asset, options give you the *right*, but not the obligation, to do so. This flexibility is what makes them so versatile. There are two basic types of options:

Call Option: The right to *buy* an asset at a specific price (the strike price) on or before a specific date (the expiration date).

Put Option: The right to *sell* an asset at a specific price (the strike price) on or before a specific date (the expiration date).

Example:

Let's say Reliance stock is currently trading at ₹2,500. You believe it will go up in the next month. You could buy a call option with a strike price of ₹2,600 expiring in one month. This gives you the right to buy Reliance at ₹2,600, even if the market price goes higher.

In Simple Terms:

Call Option: A bet that the price will go *up*.

Put Option: A bet that the price will go *down*.

4.2 Understanding Exchange-Traded Options Contracts

Just like futures, options contracts have specific terms that define the agreement:

Here in this example, I am planning to purchase put option of Bank Nifty expiring at 27 March 2025, strike price at 47000 and lot size of 30 , a price of 34.80) , if Bank Nifty will go down, I will get benefit.

Underlying Asset: The asset that you have the right to buy or sell (e.g. Here it is Bank Nifty)

Strike Price: The price at which you can buy (call option) or sell (put option) the underlying asset.(e.g. Here it is 47000)

Expiration Date: The last day on which you can exercise your option. (e.g. Here it is 27 March 2025)

Contract Size: The number of shares covered by one option contract (e.g.,Here quantity lot is 30).

Premium: The price you pay to buy the option contract. This is your maximum possible loss if the option expires worthless.(eg. Here it is Rs 34.80)

4.3 Moneyness: ITM, ATM, OTM Explained

"Moneyness" refers to the relationship between the strike price of an option and the current market price of the underlying asset. It tells you whether the option would be profitable to exercise *right now*.

OPTION	IN THE MONEY	AT THE MONEY	OUT OF THE MONEY
CALL OPTION	STOCK PRICE > STRIKE PRICE	STOCK PRICE = STRIKE PRICE	STOCK PRICE < STRIKE PRICE
PUT OPTION	STOCK PRICE < STRIKE PRICE	STOCK PRICE = STRIKE PRICE	STOCK PRICE > STRIKE PRICE

Consider that the market price of stock A is ₹200.

CALL (CE)	Strike price	PUT (PE)
In the Money	160	Out the Money
	170	
	180	
	190	
At the Money	200	At the Money
Out the Money	210	In the Money
	220	
	230	
	240	

In-the-Money (ITM): An option that would be profitable to exercise immediately.

Call Option: The market price is *above* the strike price.

Put Option: The market price is *below* the strike price.

At-the-Money (ATM): The market price is approximately *equal* to the strike price.

Out-of-the-Money (OTM): An option that would *not* be profitable to exercise immediately.

Call Option: The market price is *below* the strike price.

Put Option: The market price is *above* the strike price.

Example:

Reliance is trading at ₹2,500.

A call option with a strike price of ₹2,400 is **In-the-Money**.

A put option with a strike price of ₹2,600 is **In-the-Money**.

A call option with a strike price of ₹2,500 is **At-the-Money**.

A call option with a strike price of ₹2,600 is **Out-of-the-Money**.

A put option with a strike price of ₹2,400 is **Out-of-the-Money**.

4.4 The Two Key Components: Intrinsic Value & Time Value

The price of an option (the premium) has two components:

Intrinsic Value: The profit you would make if you exercised the option *immediately*. Only in-the-money options have intrinsic value.

Time Value: The portion of the premium that reflects the potential for the option to become more valuable before expiration. This is based on factors like time remaining until expiration, volatility of the underlying asset, and interest rates.

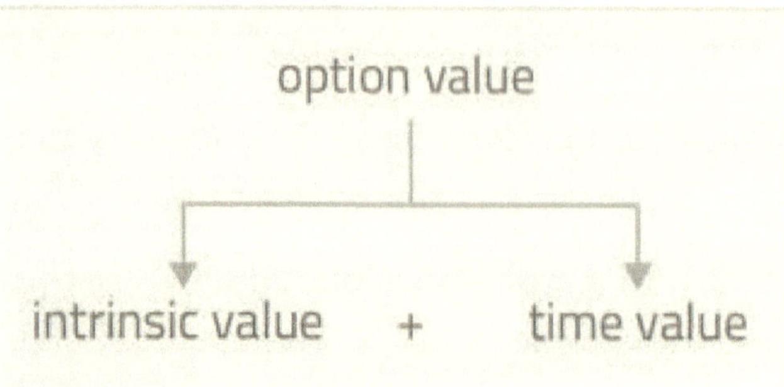

Formula:

Premium = Intrinsic Value + Time Value

Example:

Reliance is trading at ₹2,500. A call option with a strike price of ₹2,400 has a premium of ₹150.

Intrinsic Value: ₹2,500 (market price) - ₹2,400 (strike price) = ₹100

Time Value: ₹150 (premium) - ₹100 (intrinsic value) = ₹50

Even out-of-the-money options have time value because there's a chance they could become in-the-money before expiration.

4.5 Visualizing Options Payoffs: Profit & Loss Scenarios

Payoff charts are a great way to visualize the potential profit or loss from buying or selling options at different price levels. Let's look at some basic examples:

1.Buying a Call Option:

Maximum Loss: The premium paid for the option.

Maximum Profit: Unlimited (theoretically, as the price of the underlying asset can rise indefinitely).

Breakeven Point: Strike Price + Premium

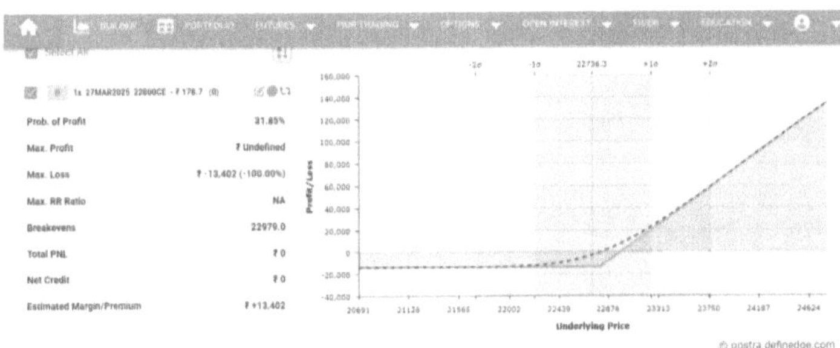

2.Buying a Put Option:

Maximum Loss: The premium paid for the option.

Maximum Profit: Strike Price (if the price of the underlying asset goes to zero).

Breakeven Point: Strike Price – Premium

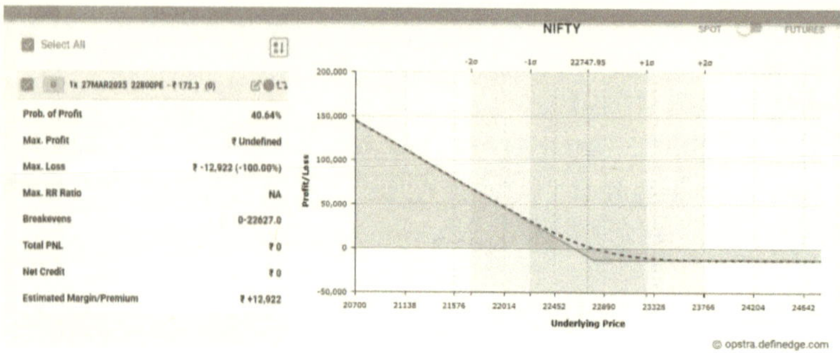

3. Selling a Call Option

Maximum Loss: Unlimited

Maximum Profit: Premium Received

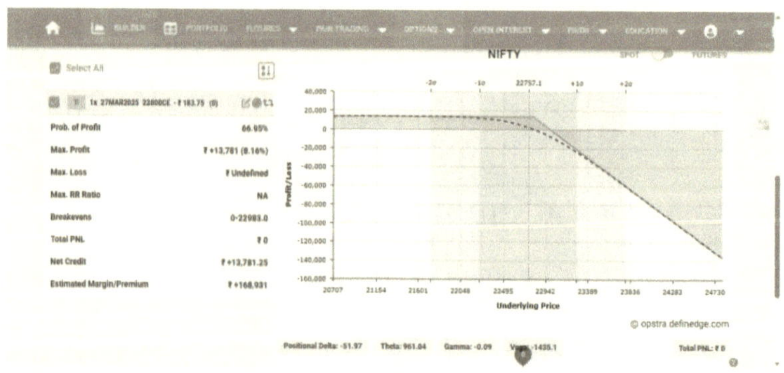

4. Selling a Put Option

Maximum Loss: Till underlying asset becomes zero

Maximum Profit: Premium Received

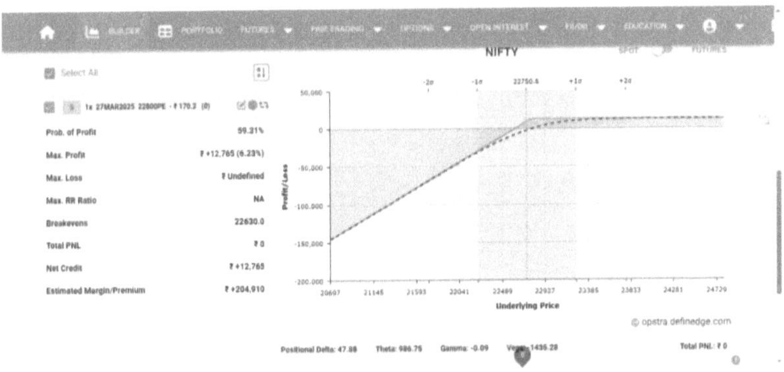

4.6 Futures vs. Options: Key Distinctions

Feature	Futures	Options
Obligation	Obligation to buy or sell	Right, but not obligation, to buy or sell
Potential Loss	Unlimited (theoretically)	Limited to the premium paid

Margin	Required	Required for sellers, not buyers
Upfront Cost	Typically no upfront cost (only margin)	Premium is paid upfront
Strategy	Directional bet	Can be used for directional bets, hedging, income generation

4.7 Option Pricing & The Role of Option Greeks

Option pricing models, like **Black-Scholes**, help calculate the **fair price** of an option by considering factors such as:

✔ The price of the asset (stock, index, etc.)

✔ Time left until expiry

✔ Market volatility

✔ Interest rates

The **"Greeks"** are important indicators that show how these factors affect an option's price. Let's understand them one by one:

Delta (Δ) – Measures Price Sensitivity

Delta shows how much the option price will change if the asset price moves by ₹1.

📌 Example: If **Delta = 0.40**, and the stock price rises by ₹1, the option price increases by ₹0.40.

- **Call options** have **positive Delta** (between 0 and 1) → they gain value when the asset price rises.
- **Put options** have **negative Delta** (between -1 and 0) → they gain value when the asset price falls.

◆ **Delta also shows the probability of the option expiring "In The Money" (ITM).**

- A **Deep ITM call option** has a **Delta close to 1.**
- A **Deep OTM option** has a **Delta close to 0.**

Gamma (Γ) – Measures Delta's Change

Gamma shows how much **Delta changes** when the asset price moves.

📌 Example: If **Gamma = 0.05**, and the stock price rises by ₹1, a **call option's Delta might change from 0.50 to 0.55.**

- **High Gamma** means Delta changes quickly, especially for **At-The-Money (ATM) options close to expiry**.
- Traders use Gamma to **adjust their positions dynamically** and hedge risks.

Theta (Θ) – Measures Time Decay

Theta shows how much an option's price drops every day as it gets closer to expiry.

📌 Example: If **Theta = -₹5**, the option price will decrease by ₹5 every day, assuming no other market changes.

- **Time decay is bad for buyers** because options lose value over time.
- **Sellers benefit from Theta**, as they earn from the "time decay" effect.

◆ **Time decay speeds up as expiry nears**.

- An option worth ₹100 with 20 days left may lose only ₹2 daily initially,
- But in the last few days, it might lose ₹10 per day.

Vega (v) – Measures Sensitivity to Volatility

Vega tells how much an option's price changes when **market volatility** changes.

📌 Example: If **Vega = ₹0.10**, and volatility increases by 1%, the option's price increases by ₹0.10.

- **Higher Vega benefits buyers** when market volatility increases (like during earnings or major news).
- **Lower Vega helps sellers**, as falling volatility reduces option prices.
- **Long-term options** have higher Vega because they are more affected by volatility shifts.

Rho (ρ) – Measures Interest Rate Impact

Rho shows how much an option's price changes when **interest rates** change.

📌 Example: If **Rho = 0.03**, and interest rates rise by **1%**, the option price increases by ₹0.03.

- **Call options have positive Rho** → Their prices increase when interest rates rise.
- **Put options have negative Rho** → Their prices decrease when interest rates rise.

◆ **Rho has the least impact** compared to other Greeks **unless interest rates change sharply**.

Why Are Greeks Important?

Understanding **option Greeks** helps traders:
✔ Manage risks effectively 🔍
✔ Choose the best option strategies 📈
✔ Adjust their positions based on market changes 💡

By using these Greeks, traders can make **better trading decisions** and improve their success in the options market! 🚀

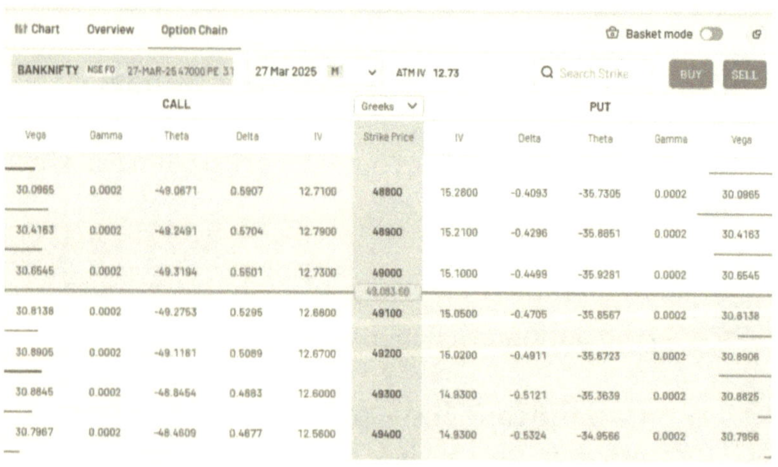

| CALL | | | | | Greeks | | PUT | | | |
Vega	Gamma	Theta	Delta	IV	Strike Price	IV	Delta	Theta	Gamma	Vega
30.0965	0.0002	-49.0671	0.5907	12.7100	48800	15.2800	-0.4093	-35.7305	0.0002	30.0965
30.4163	0.0002	-49.2491	0.5704	12.7900	48900	15.2100	-0.4296	-35.8851	0.0002	30.4163
30.6545	0.0002	-49.3194	0.5501	12.7300	49000	15.1000	-0.4499	-35.9281	0.0002	30.6545
					49,083.60					
30.8138	0.0002	-49.2753	0.5295	12.6800	49100	15.0500	-0.4705	-35.8567	0.0002	30.8138
30.8905	0.0002	-49.1181	0.5089	12.6700	49200	15.0200	-0.4911	-35.6723	0.0002	30.8906
30.8845	0.0002	-48.8454	0.4883	12.6000	49300	14.9300	-0.5121	-35.3639	0.0002	30.8825
30.7967	0.0002	-48.4609	0.4677	12.5600	49400	14.9300	-0.5324	-34.9566	0.0002	30.7956

4.8 Option Pricing Models

Black-Scholes Model: A mathematical model that uses various inputs such as strike price, current stock price, time to expiration, volatility, and risk-free interest rate to determine the theoretical value of an option.

Black-Scholes Model Formula

$$C = SN(d_1) - Ke^{-rt} N(d_2)$$

where:

$$d_1 = \frac{\ln\frac{S}{K} + \left(r + \frac{\sigma_s^2}{2}\right)t}{\sigma_s\sqrt{t}}$$

$$d_2 = d_1 - \sigma_s\sqrt{t}$$

C = Call option price

S = Current stock price

K = Strike price

r = Risk-free interest rate

t = Time to maturity

N = Normal distribution

4.9 Implied Volatility: How It Affects Your Trades

Implied volatility (IV) is the market's estimate of how much the underlying asset is expected to fluctuate in the future. It's derived from the prices of options contracts. High IV suggests that the market expects large price swings, while low IV suggests more stability. Traders use IV to gauge market sentiment and identify potentially overvalued or undervalued options.

4.10 Options Trading from a Buyer vs. Seller Perspective

Perspective	Advantages	Disadvantages
Buyer	Limited risk (maximum loss is the premium), unlimited profit potential	Time decay (theta), can lose the entire premium if wrong

| Seller | Earn premium income | Unlimited risk (theoretically), requires margin, complex strategies |

Conclusion

Options trading offers traders flexibility, allowing them to profit in different market conditions while managing risk. Unlike futures, options provide the right—but not the obligation—to buy or sell an asset. Understanding key concepts like moneyness, intrinsic value, and time value helps traders make better decisions. Payoff charts simplify profit and loss scenarios, while pricing models and implied volatility impact trade outcomes. Whether as a buyer or seller, knowing how options work is essential for success. By mastering these basics, traders can use options effectively to hedge risks, generate income, and take advantage of market movements.

Chapter 5: Winning Strategies with Futures & Options

Arun- I want to learn different strategies of Derivatives

Ravi – Definitely, there are various strategies based on Hedging, Speculation and Arbitrage. Lets start

5.1 Hedging, Speculation & Arbitrage with Futures

Think of the **stock market** as a **chessboard**. Stocks are like **pawns**, while **futures and options** are your **powerful pieces** – knights, bishops, rooks, and the queen. These tools allow you to execute **smart strategies**, **protect your investments**, and **increase your potential returns**.

But just like in **chess**, you need to understand the **rules and possible moves** to play well. This chapter will guide you in using **equity futures and options** to build **winning strategies**.

Hedging: Protecting Your Portfolio

Hedging is like **buying insurance** for your investments. If you own stocks and fear a **market downturn**, you can use **futures contracts** to reduce your risk.

📌 **Example:**

- You own **₹10 lakhs worth of Reliance shares** but are worried about a **market correction**.
- To **protect your investment**, you sell **NIFTY 50 futures contracts**.
- If the market **falls**, your Reliance shares will **lose value**, but your **futures contract will gain**.
- The **profit from the futures contract** will **offset some of your losses**, just like an **insurance payout**.

✅ **Result:** You **reduce your risk** and protect your portfolio from major losses.

Speculation: Betting on Market Direction

Speculation is about taking a **calculated risk** to **profit from price movements**. It is **riskier than hedging**, but if done correctly, the rewards can be high.

📌 **Example:**

- You expect **Infosys stock** to rise in the next month.
- You **buy Infosys futures contracts** instead of buying the stock directly.
- If **Infosys stock rises**, your **futures contract will increase in value**, and you will **make a profit**.
- However, if Infosys stock **falls**, you will **lose money**.

✅ **Result:** Speculation is a high-risk, high-reward strategy that requires **market knowledge and timing**.

Arbitrage: Risk-Free Profit from Price Differences

Arbitrage is like **finding a ₹2000 note being sold for ₹1900** and **instantly selling it for ₹2000** to make a **risk-free ₹100 profit**. It involves **exploiting price differences** between two markets.

📌 **Example:**

- Suppose **NIFTY 50 futures** are trading at a **higher price** than the actual **NIFTY 50 index**.
- An arbitrageur can **buy NIFTY 50 stocks** in the **cash market** and **sell NIFTY 50 futures contracts** at the higher price.

- As the **expiry date** nears, the **price difference will reduce**, and the arbitrageur will **lock in a risk-free profit**.

✅ **Result:** Arbitrage helps **traders earn money without taking market risk**.

Conclusion

Futures contracts are **powerful tools** that can be used for:

✔ **Hedging** → To **protect** your investments 📈
✔ **Speculation** → To **profit** from price movements 📊

✔ **Arbitrage** → To **earn risk-free returns** ⚖️

By understanding how to use futures **wisely**, you can **reduce risk, maximize profits, and make smarter trading decisions!** 🚀

5.2 Profitable Option Trading & Hedging Strategies

Options offer more flexibility than **futures**, allowing traders to use different strategies for **profit and risk management**. Let's explore some of the most **effective option trading strategies** in simple terms.

Buying Calls: The Bullish Bet 📈

A **call option** gives you the **right to buy** an asset at a fixed price before expiry. This strategy is used when you expect the price to **rise significantly**.

📌 **Example:**

- **Tata Motors** is currently at **₹500**, and you expect it to **rise sharply** due to a new product launch.
- You buy a **call option** with a **strike price of ₹520**, expiring in **one month**, for a **premium of ₹10**.
- If **Tata Motors rises above ₹530** (₹520 + ₹10), you **make a profit**.
- If it **stays below ₹520**, you **lose only ₹10 per share** (your premium).

✅ **Best for:** Traders who are confident about an **upward move** in the stock price.

Buying Puts: The Bearish Bet 📉

A **put option** gives you the **right to sell** an asset at a fixed price before expiry. This is useful when you expect the price to **drop sharply**.

📌 **Example:**

- **ICICI Bank** is currently at **₹800**, and you expect it to **fall** due to concerns over **rising bad loans (NPAs)**.
- You buy a **put option** with a **strike price of ₹780**, expiring in **one month**, for a **premium of ₹8**.
- If **ICICI Bank falls below ₹772** (₹780 - ₹8), you **make a profit**.
- If it **stays above ₹780**, you **lose only ₹8 per share** (your premium).

☑ **Best for:** Traders who want to **profit from falling stock prices**.

Covered Call: Earning Extra Income 💰

A **covered call** is a strategy where you **own shares** of a stock and **sell a call option** on those shares. This helps you **earn income (premium)** but limits your profit if the stock rises too much.

📌 **Example:**

- You own **1,000 shares of HDFC Bank** (current price ₹1,700).
- You don't expect a big price increase soon.

- You sell a **call option** with a **strike price of ₹1,750**, expiring in **one month**, for a **premium of ₹20 per share**.
- You earn **₹20 × 1,000 = ₹20,000** in premium.

✅ **If HDFC Bank stays below ₹1,750, you keep the premium and your shares.**
❌ **If HDFC Bank rises above ₹1,750,** you must **sell your shares at ₹1,750**, limiting your profit.

✅ **Best for:** Investors who **own stocks** and want to **generate extra income** while reducing risk.

Protective Put: Insurance for Your Portfolio 🛡️

A **protective put** helps you **protect your investment** if the stock price **falls**. It works like **insurance** against losses.

📌 **Example:**

- You own **200 shares of TCS**, currently at **₹3,800**.
- You fear a market correction in the **IT sector**.
- You buy a **put option** with a **strike price of ₹3,700**, expiring in **one month**, for a **premium of ₹30 per share**.

☑ **If TCS stock falls below ₹3,700**, your put option **gains value**, reducing your losses.
☑ **If TCS stock rises, you only lose the ₹30 premium** but keep your shares.

☑ **Best for:** Investors who want **protection from big losses** in their stocks.

Straddle: Profiting from Volatility 🔄

A **straddle** is used when you **expect big price movements** in a stock but don't know whether the price will go **up or down**.

📌 **Example:**

- **Bharat Forge** is currently at **₹800**, and you expect a **big price move after earnings** but **don't know if it will be good or bad**.
- You **buy both a call option and a put option** with the **same strike price of ₹800** and the **same expiry date**.
- If Bharat Forge **rises sharply**, your **call option makes a profit**.
- If Bharat Forge **falls sharply**, your **put option makes a profit**.
- If the price **does not move much**, you **lose the premium paid for both options**.

✅ **Best for:** Traders who **expect high volatility** but are **uncertain about the direction.**

Iron Condor: Earning Steady Profits from Low Volatility 📊

An **iron condor** is a strategy for when you expect a **stock to stay within a range**. It involves selling both a **call spread and a put spread** to **collect premium**.

📌 Example:

- **NIFTY 50 is at 20,000**, and you expect it to stay **between 19,800 and 20,200** for the next month.
- You sell a **call option at 20,200** and buy a **call option at 20,300**.
- You sell a **put option at 19,800** and buy a **put option at 19,700**.
- You receive **premium from both options**, and if **NIFTY stays in the range**, you **keep the entire profit**.

✅ **Best for:** Traders who expect **low market volatility** and want to earn steady profits.

Bull Put Spread: Profiting with Limited Risk in a Bullish Market 📈

A **bull put spread** is used when you expect the **market to go up slightly**. You sell a **put option at a higher strike price** and buy a **put option at a lower strike price** to **limit risk**.

📌 **Example:**

- **Infosys is at ₹1,500**, and you expect it to **stay above ₹1,450**.
- You **sell a put option at ₹1,450** and **buy a put option at ₹1,400**.
- If Infosys **stays above ₹1,450**, you keep the premium as profit.
- If Infosys **falls below ₹1,400**, your **loss is limited** due to the lower strike put.

✅ **Best for:** Traders who want **steady profits with limited risk** in a mildly bullish market.

Conclusion

Options trading offers many strategies for **profit and risk management:**

✔ **Buying Calls** → Profit from rising stock prices 📈
✔ **Buying Puts** → Profit from falling stock prices 📉
✔ **Covered Call** → Earn extra income from stocks

you already own 💰

✔ **Protective Put** → Protect your investments from big losses 🛡

✔ **Straddle** → Profit from high volatility 🔄

✔ **Iron Condor** → Earn profits when the stock moves in a range 📊

✔ **Bull Put Spread** → Profit from a mildly bullish market with limited risk ✅

By understanding and using these strategies wisely, traders can **reduce risk, maximize gains, and make better trading decisions!** 🚀

5.3 Arbitrage & The Put-Call Parity Explained

Arbitrage is a trading strategy that takes advantage of **price differences** in different markets to earn a **risk-free profit**. One of the key concepts related to arbitrage in options trading is **Put-Call Parity**.

What is Put-Call Parity?

Put-Call Parity is a mathematical relationship between the prices of **European call and put options** with the **same strike price and expiration date**. It helps in identifying **mispricing in the options market** and finding **arbitrage opportunities**.

The formula for Put-Call Parity is:

$$C - P = S - K e^{-rt}$$

Where:

- **C** = Price of the European Call Option
- **P** = Price of the European Put Option
- **S** = Current Stock Price
- **K** = Strike Price
- **r** = Risk-Free Interest Rate
- **t** = Time to Expiration

This equation ensures that the relationship between put and call options remains balanced. If the equation is violated, traders can **exploit the price difference** through arbitrage.

🎯 What is Put-Call Parity?

Imagine you want to bet on a stock (say, Infosys) going up or down. You have two tools:

- **Call option** = A ticket that gives you the right to **buy** Infosys at a fixed price in the future.
- **Put option** = A ticket that gives you the right to **sell** Infosys at a fixed price in the future.

Now, **Put-Call Parity** is like a rule that says:

"If two people have different combinations of these options and stock, but they lead to the same outcome in the future, then they should cost the same today."

If not, one is overpriced or underpriced — and that's a chance to make **risk-free profit**, which is called **arbitrage**.

◣ The Simple Formula

The rule is written like this:

Call Price - Put Price = Stock Price - Strike Price

(We skip the interest rate here to keep it super simple.)

If this balance is disturbed, you can make money without taking any risk. Let's see how.

🧿 Arbitrage Example (Easy Version)

Let's say:

- Infosys stock = ₹1,510
- Call option (₹1,500 strike) = ₹60
- Put option (₹1,500 strike) = ₹80

Now let's apply the simple formula:

Call - Put = Stock - Strike
60 - 80 = 1,510 - 1,500
−20 ≠ +10

✸ The left side and right side don't match. That means there's a pricing mismatch.

😬 How to Make Profit (Arbitrage Steps):

1. **Buy the Call** for ₹60
2. **Sell the Put** for ₹80
3. **Buy the Stock** at ₹1,510

👉 Your net cost today:

- Call (paid): ₹60
- Put (received): ₹80
- Stock (paid): ₹1,510
  Net outflow = 60 - 80 + 1,510 = ₹1,490

But in the future, whatever happens, you'll be able to **sell or buy Infosys at ₹1,500**, thanks to the options.

So you **paid ₹1,490**, but you're guaranteed to get back ₹1,500 — a ₹10 **risk-free profit**.

🪙 Final Thought:

Put-Call Parity is just a balance rule. If the balance is off, smart traders can jump in and earn a no-risk profit. It's like seeing gold selling for ₹55,000 in one shop and ₹56,000 in another — you buy from one and sell to the other.

5.4 Delta Hedging: A Trader's Secret Weapon

Delta Hedging is a strategy used to **neutralize the risk** of price movements in an options position.

What is Delta?

Delta (Δ) measures how much the price of an **option changes** when the price of the **underlying stock** moves by ₹1.

✅ **Delta values range from:**

- **Call Options:** Between **0 and +1** (Delta increases as the stock price rises).
- **Put Options:** Between **0 and -1** (Delta decreases as the stock price rises).

📌 **Example:**

- If an Infosys call option has a **delta of 0.6**, it means if Infosys stock **rises by ₹10**, the call option's price will **increase by ₹6**.
- If an Infosys put option has a **delta of -0.4**, it means if Infosys stock **falls by ₹10**, the put option's price will **increase by ₹4**.

What is Delta Hedging?

Delta Hedging is used to create a **delta-neutral portfolio** that is not affected by small price movements in the stock.

📌 How It Works:

- If you **buy a call option (Delta = +0.6)**, you can hedge the risk by **shorting 60 shares of the stock**.
- If the stock price rises, the **call option gains value**, but the **short stock position loses value**, keeping the overall profit/loss neutral.
- If the stock price falls, the **call option loses value**, but the **short stock position gains value**, again keeping the trade neutral.

✅ Delta Hedging Strategy:

- **For Long Call:** Short the stock to hedge.
- **For Long Put:** Buy the stock to hedge.
- **For Options Sellers:** Adjust positions to maintain neutrality.

📌 Example:

You buy **5 NIFTY call options** with a **delta of 0.5** each. The total delta is:

$$5 \times 0.5 = 2.55 \times 0.5 = 2.5$$

To hedge, you would **short sell 2.5 lots of NIFTY futures**, ensuring that any price movement does not affect your overall position.

Why Use Delta Hedging?

☑ **Reduces risk** from small price fluctuations.
☑ Helps traders **maintain a stable portfolio**.
☑ Used by professional traders and market makers to **protect profits**.

📢 **Key Takeaway:**
Delta hedging is a **powerful tool** that traders use to **protect themselves from sudden price movements**. However, it requires **constant adjustments** to remain effective. If done correctly, it can **reduce risk and provide stability** in options trading.

Conclusion

☑ **Put-Call Parity** helps traders **identify mispricing** and find **arbitrage opportunities**.
☑ **Delta Hedging** is used to **neutralize risk** and manage **options positions effectively**.

By understanding and using these advanced strategies, traders can **enhance their trading decisions and manage risk more effectively**. 🚀

| CALLS | | | | | | | | | | STRIKE |
OI	CHNG IN OI	VOLUME	IV	LTP	CHNG	BID QTY	BID	ASK	ASK QTY	
4,458	-756	13,171	8.10	445.65	146.90	225	442.75	443.90	150	22,950.00
96,115	-4,396	1,01,59[illegible]	8.97	398.65	[illegible]	75	398.80	399.65	150	23,000.00
7,562	-4,457	56,724	9.48	356.70	132.25	225	356.90	357.65	75	23,050.00
47,548	-3,264	3,09,759	9.91	315.90	124.35	75	316.30	317.00	300	23,100.00
20,011	4,375	4,06,907	9.99	278.80	116.85	675	277.90	278.60	750	23,150.00
78,994	6,671	11,08,839	10.28	242.00	107.20	225	241.65	242.00	75	23,200.00
26,473	8,443	8,18,253	10.41	208.35	98.05	600	208.00	208.35	225	23,250.00
76,590	29,708	14,12,063	10.53	176.60	87.70	75	176.50	176.75	525	23,300.00
42,853	29,508	8,63,714	10.59	148.20	77.90	900	148.20	148.50	750	23,350.00
71,675	11,221	10,66,712	10.58	122.80	68.45	750	122.50	122.60	375	23,400.00

Understanding Open Interest and Put-Call Ratio in Options Trading

Options and futures trading can be complex, but two important indicators—**Open Interest (OI) and Put-Call Ratio (PCR)**—help traders understand market activity and sentiment. Let's break them down in **simple terms** to help you make better trading decisions.

5.5 What is Open Interest (OI)?

✅ **Definition:**
Open Interest (OI) is the total number of **outstanding (open) futures or options contracts** in the market. It shows how much activity is happening in a particular contract.

✅ **Why is it Important?**

- **Rising OI** → More traders are entering new positions, showing **strong interest and liquidity** in that contract.
- **Falling OI** → Traders are **closing their positions**, meaning interest in that contract is decreasing.

✅ How to Use Open Interest?

- **OI increasing + Price increasing** → **Bullish signal** (More buyers are entering, expecting the price to rise).
- **OI increasing + Price decreasing** → **Bearish signal** (More sellers are entering, expecting the price to fall).
- **OI decreasing + Price increasing** → **Weak bullish trend** (Short covering rally, not strong buying).
- **OI decreasing + Price decreasing** → **Weak bearish trend** (Long unwinding, traders booking profits).

📌 Example:

Imagine **Reliance Industries** is trading at ₹2,500, and the OI in its **call options** is rising. This suggests that more traders are **buying call options**, expecting the stock price to rise. If OI rises sharply, it confirms that **big investors (FIIs, DIIs) are involved,** making the trend stronger.

What is the Put-Call Ratio (PCR)?

☑ **Definition:**
Put-Call Ratio (PCR) is the ratio of **put options traded to call options traded**. It helps traders understand **market sentiment** (whether traders are more bullish or bearish).

☑ **Formula:**

PCR=Total Puts Open Interest\Total Calls Open Interest

☑ **How to Interpret PCR?**

- **PCR > 1** → More puts than calls → Market is **bearish** (Traders are buying more put options, expecting prices to fall).
- **PCR < 1** → More calls than puts → Market is **bullish** (Traders are buying more call options, expecting prices to rise).
- **PCR around 1** → Balanced market (No strong trend).

☑ **Contrarian Trading with PCR:**
Sometimes, extreme PCR values can signal **trend reversals**:

- **Very High PCR (above 1.3-1.5)** → Too many put options → **Market may be oversold and ready to bounce back.**

- **Very Low PCR (below 0.7-0.8)** → Too many call options → **Market may be overbought and ready to correct**.

📌 Example:

If **NIFTY 50's PCR is above 1**, it means more traders are buying put options, expecting a market fall. However, if the PCR is **too high (e.g., 1.5)**, it could mean **panic selling**, and a **bounce-back rally may happen**. On the other hand, if the **PCR is very low (e.g., 0.6)**, it may indicate **excessive bullishness**, and a **market correction may follow**.

How to Use OI and PCR Together?

✅ **OI increasing + PCR above 1.3 → Too much fear → Possible market reversal upwards**.
✅ **OI increasing + PCR below 0.7 → Too much greed → Possible market correction downwards**.
✅ **OI stable + PCR around 1 → No clear trend, wait for confirmation**.

Final Thoughts

Open Interest (OI) shows the strength of market participation, while **Put-Call Ratio (PCR)** helps gauge overall sentiment. By **understanding and combining these indicators**, you can make more informed decisions in **equity derivatives trading**.

 But remember: Options trading is risky, and market conditions can change quickly. Always consider your **risk tolerance and investment goals** before taking positions. **Use stop-loss and risk management strategies to protect your capital!**

Conclusion

Futures and options are powerful tools when used with the right strategies. Traders can hedge risks, speculate on price movements, or take advantage of arbitrage opportunities. Understanding put-call parity helps in identifying mispriced options, while delta hedging allows traders to manage risk effectively. Open interest (OI) provides valuable insights into market trends and trader positions. By mastering these strategies, traders can improve their decision-making and increase profitability. Success in derivatives trading comes from knowledge, discipline, and the ability to apply the right strategy at the right time.

Chapter 6: The Trading Playbook – How Markets Function

Imagine you're walking onto the trading floor of a stock exchange – or, more likely, logging into your trading account online. You've learned about futures and options, but how do you actually *buy* and *sell* them? What happens behind the scenes? This chapter pulls back the curtain on the trading mechanism of equity derivatives in India, explaining the processes, rules, and costs involved.

6.1 The Trading Mechanism Uncovered

Trading equity derivatives isn't as simple as buying a stock. Here's a simplified overview of the process:

Opening a Demat and Trading Account:

Just like trading stocks, you need a Demat (Dematerialized) account to hold your derivatives positions electronically and a trading account to place your orders.

Example: You can open a Demat and trading account with brokers like Zerodha, Upstox, ICICI Direct, or HDFC Securities.

Margin Requirements:

Derivatives trading involves leverage, meaning you control a large position with a relatively small amount of capital. Therefore, you need to deposit margin with your broker. This acts as collateral to cover potential losses.

Example: If you want to buy one lot of NIFTY futures, which has a contract value of, say, ₹12 lakhs, you might need to deposit an initial margin of ₹1.5 lakhs with your broker. This margin varies based on volatility and exchange rules.

Placing an Order:

You can place orders through your broker's online platform, trading app, or by calling them directly. You specify the contract you want to trade (e.g., NIFTY 50 futures, Reliance call option), the quantity (number of lots), the price (or order type), and the order validity.

Example: You want to buy one lot of NIFTY 50 futures expiring in the current month. You can place a "market order" to buy at the best available price, or a "limit order" to buy only if the price falls to a certain level.

Order Matching:

The exchange's trading system matches buy and sell orders based on price and time priority. This means the order with the best price and earliest time stamp gets executed first.

Example: The National Stock Exchange (NSE) uses a fully automated, screen-based trading system to match orders.

Execution and Confirmation:

Once your order is matched, it's executed, and you receive a confirmation from your broker. This confirmation includes details like the contract traded, the price, and the quantity.

Example: You'll receive an email and SMS confirmation from your broker immediately after your order is executed.

Mark-to-Market (MTM):

Futures positions are marked-to-market daily. This means the profits or losses on your position are calculated based on the daily settlement price, and your margin account is adjusted accordingly.

Example: If you bought NIFTY futures and the NIFTY rises, your margin account will be credited with the profit at the end of the day. If the NIFTY falls, your margin account will be debited with the loss. If your margin balance falls below the required level, you'll receive a margin call and need to deposit additional funds.

Expiration and Settlement:

Futures and options contracts expire on a specific date. On the expiration date, the contracts are settled. This can happen through physical delivery (for some stock futures) or cash settlement (for most index futures and options).

Example: NIFTY 50 futures and options contracts expire on the last Thursday of the month. On the expiration date, the contracts are cash-settled based on the final settlement price.

6.2 Which Stocks Qualify for Derivatives Trading?

Not all stocks are available for trading in the derivatives market. Exchanges have specific criteria for selecting stocks for inclusion in the derivatives segment. These criteria are designed to ensure liquidity, market depth, and investor protection. Key factors include:

Market Capitalization: The stock must have a sufficiently high market capitalization.

Liquidity: The stock must be actively traded in the cash market, with a high trading volume.

Free Float: A significant portion of the company's shares must be available for trading by the public (not held by promoters or government).

Price Volatility: The stock's price volatility should be within acceptable limits.

6.3 The Selection Criteria for Index-Based Trading

Similar to stocks, not every index is eligible for derivatives trading. The selection criteria for indices include:

Representativeness: The index should accurately represent the market segment it's designed to track.

Diversification: The index should be well-diversified across different sectors and companies.

Liquidity: The constituent stocks of the index should be actively traded.

Market Capitalization: The index should have a high overall market capitalization.

6.4 How Corporate Actions Impact Derivatives Trading

Corporate actions, such as dividends, stock splits, bonus issues, and mergers, can affect the value of derivatives contracts. Exchanges make adjustments to the contract terms to ensure that the economic value of the contracts remains unchanged.

Dividends: For stock futures, the futures price is adjusted downwards by the expected dividend amount.

Stock Splits and Bonus Issues: The contract size is adjusted to reflect the increased number of shares.

Mergers and Acquisitions: The contract may be replaced with a new contract based on the merged entity.

Example: If a company announces a bonus issue of 1:1 (one bonus share for every share held), the contract size of the futures contract will be doubled.

6.5 Trading Costs: What You Need to Know

Trading derivatives involves various costs:

Brokerage: Commission charged by the broker for executing the trade.

Exchange Transaction Charges: Fees charged by the stock exchange.

Securities Transaction Tax (STT): Tax levied by the government on certain transactions.

Goods and Services Tax (GST): Tax levied on brokerage and exchange transaction charges.

SEBI Fees: Fees charged by the Securities and Exchange Board of India (SEBI).

Stamp Duty: Tax levied on transfer documents.

It's important to factor in all these costs when calculating the profitability of your trades.

6.6 Algorithmic Trading: The Future of Markets

Algorithmic trading (also known as algo trading) involves using computer programs to automatically execute trades based on predefined rules and parameters. This allows for faster execution, reduced human error, and the ability to implement complex trading strategies.

6.7 Decoding Futures & Options Data for Smarter Trades

Tracking data such as price, open interest, and trading volume is crucial for making informed trading decisions. Websites like the NSE (National Stock Exchange) and BSE (Bombay Stock Exchange), as well as financial data providers like Reuters and Bloomberg, provide real-time and historical data on equity derivatives.

6.8 Understanding Investor Risk Reduction Access (IRRA)

IRRA platform is introduced by exchanges to reduce risk for investors. In case of technical glitch faced by Trading Member, the investors can directly place order through IRRA platform.

By understanding the trading mechanism, eligibility criteria, adjustments for corporate actions, and trading costs, you can navigate the derivatives market more effectively. Always remember to trade responsibly and manage your risk carefully. Happy Trading!

Conclusion

Understanding how markets function is crucial for successful derivatives trading. Not all stocks qualify for derivatives trading, and strict selection criteria apply, especially for index-based trading. Corporate actions like dividends and stock splits can impact derivatives prices. Traders must also consider trading costs, which affect profitability. Algorithmic trading is shaping the future of markets, making trades faster and more efficient. Analyzing futures and options data helps in making smarter trading decisions. Additionally, Investor Risk Reduction Access (IRRA) plays a role in managing risks. By mastering these concepts, traders can navigate the market with confidence and better strategies.

Chapter 7: Clearing & Settlement – Behind the Scenes of Every Trade

Can Options Give Physical Delivery of Shares?

Arun: Can options give physical delivery of shares? If I bought in-the-money (ITM) Reliance Industries call options, what will happen on the last day of expiry?

Ravi: Yes, Arun! If you hold an **ITM call option** for **Reliance Industries** until the expiry date, you will receive **physical delivery** of shares unless you close your position before expiry. Let me explain how this works.

Physical Delivery of Shares in Stock Options

1. Mandatory Physical Settlement (SEBI Rules)

- In **India**, as per **SEBI regulations**, all **stock options** that are **in the money (ITM) on expiry day** are **settled physically**.

- This means that instead of receiving cash, you will **receive the actual shares** in your **demat account** if you hold ITM call options at expiry.

2. What Happens on Expiry Day?

If you **do not sell your ITM call option before expiry**, your broker will automatically exercise it. This means:

- You will **receive 100 shares** of **Reliance Industries per lot** at the **strike price** you chose.
- The seller (option writer) must **deliver the shares to your demat account**.
- Your brokerage will process the transaction based on your available funds.

☑ **Example:**

- You bought a **Reliance Industries ₹2,500 Call Option** for **1 lot (100 shares)**.
- On expiry day, the stock price is **₹2,600** (ITM).
- Since the stock price is **above your strike price**, your call option is exercised.
- You **must pay ₹2,500 per share** (total **₹2,50,000**) to receive the **100 shares** in your **demat account**.

3. Important Things to Keep in Mind

💡 **Demat Account Requirement:**

- Ensure that your **demat account** is active because the shares will be delivered there.

💰 **Sufficient Funds Needed:**

- You **must have enough money** in your trading account to pay for the shares at the **strike price**.
- If you **do not have enough funds**, your broker may buy the shares and sell them immediately, passing on any **profit or loss** to you.

📉 **Out-of-the-Money (OTM) Options Expire Worthless:**

- If your call option **is OTM** (for example, Reliance closes at **₹2,490** while your strike price is ₹2,500), it will **expire worthless**.
- You will **lose the premium paid** for the option, but there will be **no physical delivery**.

---

4. How to Avoid Physical Delivery?

If you **do not want to receive shares**, you should **sell your ITM call option before expiry**.

📌 **Why Sell Before Expiry?**

- You can **book profits** without needing to **buy the shares**.
- You **avoid the need for a large amount of money** for physical settlement.
- You **protect yourself from last-minute price fluctuations**.

Conclusion

☑ **If your call option is ITM on expiry day**, you will **receive physical delivery** of shares.
☑ **Make sure you have enough funds** in your account to settle the trade.
☑ If you **don't want to take delivery, exit your position before expiry**.

Arun: Thank you so much! Now I understand.
Ravi: You're welcome! Let's move to the next topic.

Clearing and Settlement in Derivatives Trading: The Backbone of Market Stability

Imagine you placed a bet on a cricket match and won. You celebrate, but how do you actually get your winnings? Who ensures that the money is transferred fairly and correctly?

In the world of **derivatives trading, clearing and settlement** play this crucial role. This behind-the-scenes process ensures that **all trades are honored, risks are managed, and the market functions smoothly**. It may sound technical, but understanding it is essential for anyone trading derivatives in **India**.

7.1 Clearing Members: The Gatekeepers of the System

Clearing members are the **backbone of the clearing and settlement process**. They act as intermediaries between **trading members (brokers) and the clearing corporation**. Think of them as **trusted guarantors** who ensure that every trade is settled properly.

Key Roles of Clearing Members

◆ **Guaranteeing Trades:**

- They guarantee the **financial obligations** of the trades they clear.
- If a trading member defaults, the clearing member is responsible for fulfilling the trade.

◆ **Managing Risk:**

- They **collect margins** from traders to cover potential losses.

- They **monitor trading activity** to ensure compliance with risk limits.

◆ **Settlement:**

- They facilitate the **transfer of funds and securities** between the buyer and seller.

Types of Clearing Members

☑ **Professional Clearing Members (PCM):**

- These are **specialized firms** that focus only on **clearing and settlement**.
- Example: Large financial institutions or dedicated clearing firms.

☑ **Trading-Cum-Clearing Members (TCM):**

- These are brokers who **both trade and clear their own trades** as well as those of their clients.
- Example: Many large brokerage houses in India.

◆ **Major Clearing Members in India:**

- **Banks like HDFC Bank and ICICI Bank**
- **Dedicated Clearing Corporations like NSCCL (National Securities Clearing Corporation Ltd.)**

7.2 The Clearing Mechanism: From Trade to Settlement

The **clearing mechanism** ensures that trades are **validated, matched, and guaranteed** before settlement. Here's how it works:

Step-by-Step Clearing Process

1 **Trade Capture:**

- When you place an order through your broker, the details of your trade are **recorded in the exchange's trading system**.

2. **Trade Confirmation:**

- Your broker (trading member) sends the trade details to their clearing member for **confirmation**.

3. **Trade Matching:**

- The clearing corporation **matches the buy and sell orders** to ensure that both parties agree on the trade.

4. **Novation (Trade Guarantee):**

- The clearing corporation **becomes the buyer to every seller and the seller to every buyer**.
- This guarantees that trades are honored **even if one party defaults**.
- This process is called **novation**, a key risk management tool.

5.Risk Management:

- The clearing corporation calculates **margin requirements** based on the trader's positions and market conditions.
- Clearing members ensure that their clients have **sufficient funds or securities** to settle the trade.

Example: How NSE's Clearing Mechanism Works

📌 **National Securities Clearing Corporation Ltd. (NSCCL)**

- NSCCL is the **clearing corporation for the National Stock Exchange (NSE)**.
- It acts as the **central counterparty for all derivatives trades on NSE**.
- It ensures that all buyers and sellers **meet their trade obligations**.

✅ **If a trader buys NIFTY futures on NSE:**

- The **exchange records the trade**.
- The **clearing member confirms it**.
- **NSCCL guarantees the trade**, ensuring that the seller delivers and the buyer pays.

Conclusion

◆ **Clearing and settlement** ensure that **all trades in derivatives markets** are executed **smoothly and securely**.

◆ **Clearing members** act as **gatekeepers** by managing **risk, ensuring settlement, and guaranteeing trades**.

◆ **The clearing mechanism (including novation)** ensures that **buyers and sellers always get what they agreed upon**.

◆ **Clearing corporations like NSCCL** play a **vital role in maintaining market integrity and reducing counterparty risk**.

Understanding these concepts will help you **trade derivatives with more confidence and clarity!**

7.3 Interoperability of Clearing Corporations: Connecting the Markets

In India, **interoperability** allows clearing members to **choose** which clearing corporation they want to use for settling their trades, **regardless of which exchange the trade was executed on**. This means that a trade executed on **NSE** can be settled through a clearing corporation linked to **BSE**, and vice versa.

Benefits of Interoperability

☑ **Reduced Costs:**

- Clearing members can **consolidate** their clearing activity with a **single clearing corporation**, reducing operational expenses.

☑ **Increased Efficiency:**

- It streamlines the clearing process, making settlements **faster and smoother**.

☑ **Enhanced Competition:**

- With multiple clearing corporations competing, services improve, and clearing fees become more competitive.

📌 **Example:**

- **SEBI has implemented interoperability in India**.
- A trading member can now **choose** to clear trades done on **BSE (Bombay Stock Exchange)** through **ICCL (Indian Clearing Corporation Limited)** or trades done on **NSE (National Stock Exchange)** through **NSCCL (National Securities Clearing Corporation Ltd.)**.

7.4 Settlement Mechanism: Delivering on the Promise

The **settlement mechanism** is the process by which the **obligations of derivatives contracts are fulfilled**. This involves the transfer of **funds and/or securities** between buyers and sellers.

Types of Settlement

1.Mark-to-Market Settlement

- This applies to **futures contracts**, where **profits and losses are settled daily**.
- Your **margin account is adjusted every day** based on the market price.

📌 **Example:**

- If you **hold a NIFTY futures contract** and **NIFTY rises**, your account is **credited daily** based on the price difference between today and yesterday.

2.Final Settlement (On Expiry Date)

◆ **Cash Settlement:**

- The most common method, where the **difference between the contract price and the final settlement price is paid in cash.**
  📌 Example:
- **NIFTY 50 futures and options** are **cash-settled**.
- If your **NIFTY 50 call option is in-the-money (ITM) on expiry**, you will receive the difference **between the settlement price and your strike price** in cash.

◆ **Physical Delivery:**

- Less common for **index derivatives** but applies to **some stock futures and options**.
- The actual **shares are delivered to the buyer or received from the seller**.

📌 **Example:**

- If you hold a **stock futures contract that requires physical delivery**, you must **deliver (if short) or receive (if long)** the specified number of shares on the settlement date.

7.5 Risk Management: Safeguarding the System

Risk management is **essential** in derivatives trading to **prevent defaults and market instability**. Clearing corporations use various tools to **reduce risks** and **protect traders and brokers**.

Key Risk Management Measures

✅ 1.Margin Requirements

Clearing corporations **collect margins** to **cover potential losses**.

📌 Types of Margin:

- **Initial Margin:** The first deposit required to open a trade.
- **Maintenance Margin:** The minimum amount that must always be maintained in the account.
- **Extreme Loss Margin:** Additional margin during extreme volatility.

☑ **2.Position Limits**

- **Limits are placed on how many contracts a clearing member can hold** to reduce excessive speculation.

☑ **3.Price Bands**

- **Daily limits** on how much a derivative's price can move, preventing **wild swings and market manipulation**.

☑ **4. Stress Testing**

- Clearing corporations **simulate extreme market scenarios** to ensure the system can handle crashes or volatility.

☑ **5. Guarantee Fund**

- A **fund created from contributions by clearing members** to cover losses in case of a default.

📌 **Example:**

- **NSCCL (NSE's clearing corporation)** uses the **SPAN (Standard Portfolio Analysis of Risk) system** to **calculate margin requirements** and manage risk efficiently.

Conclusion

◆ **Interoperability** in clearing corporations **reduces costs, increases efficiency, and boosts competition**.

◆ **The settlement mechanism** ensures that **traders receive their profits or securities on time**.

◆ **Risk management strategies** like **margin requirements, position limits, and stress testing** keep the **market safe and stable**.

Understanding these concepts will help you **trade derivatives in India with confidence and security!**

7.6 Margining and Mark-to-Market under SPAN

SPAN (Standard Portfolio Analysis of Risk) is a widely used risk management system in India, adopted by **NSCCL (National Securities Clearing Corporation Ltd.)** to calculate margin requirements for derivatives trading.

Key Features of SPAN:

☑ **Portfolio-Based Approach** – SPAN calculates margins based on the entire portfolio, considering how different assets interact.

☑ **Scenario Analysis** – It simulates multiple market conditions to estimate the worst possible loss.

☑ **Volatility Scans** – Margin requirements adjust dynamically based on market volatility.

☑ **Mark-to-Market (MTM)** – Every day, all positions are settled at the latest market price, and margins are adjusted accordingly.

How SPAN Works (Simplified):

1. **Portfolio Input** – Traders input their positions into the SPAN system.
2. **Scenario Generation** – SPAN tests different price and volatility changes.
3. **Loss Calculation** – The system calculates potential losses under each scenario.
4. **Margin Requirement** – The highest possible loss determines the margin a trader must maintain.

📌 **Example:** If you trade **NIFTY futures and stock options**, SPAN calculates a **single margin** for your portfolio instead of separate margins for each trade.

Understanding SPAN helps traders manage risk effectively and ensures financial stability in the derivatives market.

7.7 Position Limits: How Much Can You Trade?

Position limits prevent excessive speculation and market manipulation in derivatives trading. **SEBI (Securities and Exchange Board of India)** has set three types of position limits in the **equity derivatives** segment.

1.Client-Level Position Limit

- A trader cannot hold more than:
  - ◆ **1% of the free-float market capitalization** of a stock, OR
  - ◆ **5% of the total open interest** in all derivative contracts of that stock.

📌 **Example:**

- If a company has **10 crore free float shares**, 1% is **10 lakh shares**.
- If the total open interest is **1 crore**, 5% is **5 lakh shares**.
- The **higher limit applies**.

2. Trading Member-Wise Position Limit

- **Index Futures & Options:** ₹7,500 crore or **15% of total open interest**, whichever is higher.

- **Individual Stocks:** Combined futures and options position cannot exceed **20% of the Market-Wide Position Limit (MWPL)**.

3. *Market-Wide Position Limits (MWPL)*

- MWPL = **20% of a company's free float shares**.
- If **open interest crosses 95% of MWPL**, new trades are banned until it falls below 80%.

📌 **Example:**

- A company with **50 crore free float shares** has an **MWPL of 10 crore shares**.
- If open interest exceeds **9.5 crore shares**, fresh positions are **blocked**.

Traders exceeding limits face penalties and trading restrictions. These rules ensure **fair trading and protect market stability**. 🚀

7.8 Violations, Penalties & Compliance Risks

Stock market participants, including **trading members** and **clearing members**, must follow strict regulations. Any rule violation can result in **penalties and disciplinary actions**.

Common Violations:

◆ **Margin & Settlement Violations** – Not maintaining required margins or failing to deliver securities on time.

◆ **Position Limit & Exposure Breaches** – Exceeding allowed trading limits.

◆ **Misuse of Client Collateral** – Using client funds or securities for unauthorized purposes.

◆ **Reporting Failures** – Incorrect or incomplete reporting of client margins.

◆ **Market-Wide Position Limit (MWPL) Violations** – Exceeding limits set by the exchange.

Consequences of Violations:

☑ **Trading rights withdrawal** without notice.

☑ **Forced closure** of outstanding positions.

☑ **Monetary penalties** or seizure of collateral.

📌 **Example:** If a trader does not maintain the required margin, the exchange can **square off their positions**, leading to **unexpected losses**.

7.9 Managing Client Funds: Settlement of Running Accounts

To **prevent misuse** of client funds, **SEBI mandates brokers** to settle accounts regularly.

☑ Funds must be **settled monthly or quarterly**, based on the client's choice.
☑ Brokers must follow a **uniform settlement schedule** set at the start of each financial year.

📌 **Example:** If a trader has ₹50,000 with a broker and no open trades, the broker must **return the amount** within the settlement cycle.

These rules ensure **transparency** and **protect traders' funds**.

7.10 The Safety Nets: Settlement Guarantee & Investor Protection Fund

Settlement Guarantee Fund (SGF):

- A **safety net** maintained by clearing corporations.
- Covers shortfalls if a clearing member **defaults**, preventing market disruptions.

Each market segment (Cash, F&O, Currency) has a **separate SGF**.

Investor Protection Fund (IPF):

- **Compensates investors** when a trading member defaults and cannot repay.
- Also funds **investor education programs**.

Recent SEBI Regulations for Market Stability:

◆ **Upfront Collection of Option Premium (Feb 1, 2025)** – Buyers must **pay the full premium** before trading to avoid excessive leverage.

◆ **No Calendar Spread Margin Benefits on Expiry Day (Feb 1, 2025)** – Full margin required for contracts expiring the same day.

◆ **Intraday Monitoring of Position Limits (Apr 1, 2025)** – Exchanges will check position limits **at least four times daily**.

◆ **Increased Contract Size (Nov 20, 2024)** – **New index derivatives** will have a minimum market value of ₹15–₹20 lakhs to **reduce speculation**.

◆ **Rationalization of Weekly Expiries (Nov 20, 2024) – Only one benchmark index** per exchange can have weekly expiry.

◆ **Extra Margin on Expiry Day (Nov 20, 2024) – Additional 2% margin** on short options to **manage volatility**.

These measures aim to **enhance market stability and investor protection**.

7.11 Cybersecurity & Risk Resilience in Stock Broking

With technology playing a **major role** in trading, **cybersecurity risks** have become a **big concern**.

To **protect investor data**, SEBI has introduced the **Cyber Security & Cyber Resilience Framework (CSCRF)** for stockbrokers and depository participants. This will be **implemented in phases from January 1, 2025**.

Key Market Participants Under CSCRF:

- Stock Exchanges
- Depositories
- Clearing Corporations
- KYC Registration Agencies (KRAs)
- Qualified Registrar and Transfer Agents (QRTAs)

Five Key Goals of Cyber Resilience:

1. **Anticipate** – Identify and prepare for potential cyber threats.
2. **Withstand** – Ensure core trading operations continue despite attacks.
3. **Contain** – Limit the damage by isolating affected systems.
4. **Recover** – Restore normal functioning quickly after an attack.

5 **Evolve** – Continuously improve security to prevent future threats.

📌 **Example:** If a stockbroker's system is hacked, CSCRF ensures that **data protection, backups, and fast recovery** measures are in place, preventing market disruptions.

These cybersecurity rules **strengthen investor confidence** and **maintain market integrity**.

Conclusion

Clearing and settlement ensure that every trade in the derivatives market is completed smoothly and securely. Clearing members act as gatekeepers, managing risks and ensuring compliance. The settlement process, whether cash or physical delivery, guarantees that obligations are met. Strong risk management measures, including SPAN margining and mark-to-market adjustments, protect the system. Position limits prevent excessive trading risks, while penalties ensure compliance. Investor protection funds and cybersecurity measures add extra layers of safety. By understanding these mechanisms, traders can gain confidence in the market's reliability and trade with greater security and efficiency.

Chapter 8: The Legal & Regulatory Framework - Rules Every Trader Must Know

Imagine a bustling marketplace, filled with traders buying and selling everything from spices to gold. Without clear rules and a governing body, chaos would quickly ensue: fraud, manipulation, and ultimately, a loss of confidence. The same applies to the equity derivatives market. Regulations are the essential "rule book" that ensures fairness, transparency, and investor protection. This chapter breaks down the key regulatory players and rules that govern the equity derivatives market in India, making it easier for you to understand the framework that protects your investments.

8.1 The Regulatory Framework: A Three-Tiered Structure

The Indian securities market, including **equity derivatives**, follows a **three-tiered regulatory structure** to ensure transparency, fairness, and investor protection.

1. Government of India

The **Government of India** is the **apex body** responsible for making laws and setting the overall **economic and legal framework** for financial markets.

◆ **Role:** Enacts laws and policies that govern the securities market.

◆ **Example:** The **Ministry of Finance** oversees the financial sector and makes key financial policies.

2. Securities and Exchange Board of India (SEBI)

SEBI is the **primary regulator** of the Indian stock market. It ensures that stock exchanges, clearing corporations, and market intermediaries follow fair and transparent practices.

◆ **Role:** Protects investors, regulates market activities, and promotes the growth of the securities market.

◆ **Example:** SEBI makes rules for **trading, clearing, settlement, and risk management** in the equity derivatives market.

3. Self-Regulatory Organizations (SROs)

SROs are organizations that regulate their own members under **SEBI's supervision**. The main SROs in the equity derivatives market are **stock exchanges and clearing corporations**.

◆ **Role:** Implement SEBI regulations, create their own trading rules, and monitor market participants.

◆ **Example:**

☑ **Stock Exchanges:** The **National Stock Exchange (NSE)** and **Bombay Stock Exchange (BSE)** set rules for trading derivatives.

☑ **Clearing Corporations: National Securities Clearing Corporation Limited (NSCCL)** and **Indian Clearing Corporation Limited (ICCL)** manage clearing and settlement risks.

This **three-tier system** ensures that the market functions smoothly and remains **safe for investors**.

8.2 SEBI: The Watchdog of Indian Stock Markets

SEBI (Securities and Exchange Board of India) is the **most powerful regulator** of the Indian stock market. Its role is to ensure that markets operate in a **fair, transparent, and efficient** manner.

Key Functions of SEBI:

◆ **1. Registration & Regulation of Market Intermediaries**

SEBI **registers and regulates** brokers, sub-brokers, clearing members, and portfolio managers to ensure ethical and qualified professionals operate in the market.

📌 **Example:** If you want to become a **broker in the derivatives market**, you must first **register with SEBI** and follow its rules.

◆ **2. Regulation of Stock Exchanges & Clearing Corporations**

SEBI **oversees** stock exchanges and clearing corporations to ensure fair trading, smooth settlement, and strong risk management.

📌 **Example:** SEBI **approves the rules of NSE and BSE** and monitors them to protect investors.

◆ **3. Prevention of Fraud & Unfair Trade Practices**

SEBI takes strict action against **insider trading, price manipulation, and market fraud** to maintain investor confidence.

📌 **Example:** If a company official **shares inside information** to profit from stock trades, SEBI can **investigate and impose heavy penalties**.

◆ **4. Investor Protection & Awareness**

SEBI works to **educate investors** about market risks and provides ways to resolve investor complaints.

📌 **Example:** SEBI runs **investor awareness programs** across India to teach people about stock and derivatives trading.

SEBI plays a **critical role** in making India's stock markets **safe, transparent, and efficient** for all participants. 🚀

8.3 Important Regulations Pertaining to Equity Derivatives

Equity derivatives trading in India is governed by a strong regulatory framework to ensure transparency, fairness, and investor protection. The Securities and Exchange Board of India (SEBI) is the main regulator, while stock exchanges like the National Stock Exchange (NSE) and Bombay Stock Exchange (BSE) also have their own rules.

Key SEBI Regulations

1. **SEBI (Prohibition of Insider Trading) Regulations**
   These rules prevent individuals with confidential, price-sensitive information from trading securities before the information becomes public.
   Example: If a company director knows about an upcoming merger, they cannot trade the company's shares or derivatives before the public announcement.
2. **SEBI (Prohibition of Fraudulent and Unfair Trade Practices) Regulations**
   These regulations stop unfair activities like market manipulation, misleading advertisements, and fake trades.

Example: Artificially increasing stock prices through coordinated trading to attract investors is illegal.

3. **SEBI (Stock Brokers) Regulations**
These rules govern stockbrokers' responsibilities, including client onboarding, margin requirements, and risk disclosures. *Example:* Brokers must give clients a risk disclosure document before they start trading in derivatives.

4. **SEBI (Research Analysts) Regulations**
Research analysts must follow ethical guidelines and disclose any conflicts of interest while giving investment recommendations. *Example:* If an analyst owns shares of a company, they must declare it before recommending the stock.

5. **SEBI Circulars and Guidelines**
SEBI frequently issues circulars to clarify existing rules and introduce new measures to address market challenges.

Exchange-Prescribed Framework

Apart from SEBI regulations, stock exchanges and clearing corporations have their own guidelines for trading and clearing derivatives. These include:

- **Trading Hours:** Equity derivatives can be traded between 9:15 AM and 3:30 PM.
- **Contract Specifications:** Rules regarding contract size, tick size, and expiry dates.

- **Margin Requirements:** Traders must maintain adequate margins to manage risks.
- **Position Limits:** A cap on the number of contracts a trader can hold.
- **Price Bands:** Limits on daily price changes to prevent excessive volatility.
- **Trading Rules:** Guidelines for order placement, matching, and execution.
- **Surveillance Mechanisms:** Exchanges monitor trading activities to detect suspicious transactions.
- **Investor Grievance Redressal:** A mechanism to resolve investor disputes.

Example: NSE and BSE regulate NIFTY 50 futures and options trading by setting rules on margins, position limits, and trading hours.

8.4 Investor Grievance Redressal

If an investor has an issue with a broker or any market participant, there are several ways to seek redressal:

1. **Internal Grievance Redressal:** First, try to resolve the issue directly with the broker.
2. **Exchange Mechanism:** If not resolved, file a complaint with NSE or BSE.
3. **SEBI Complaints Redress System (SCORES):** Investors can lodge complaints online and track their status.
4. **Arbitration:** If no resolution is reached, the case can be taken to arbitration.

Example: If a broker fails to execute an order properly or charges excessive brokerage fees, the investor can file a complaint through the SCORES platform.

8.5 Prohibited Activities in Equity Derivatives

SEBI strictly prohibits certain unfair practices in the derivatives market, including:

- **Insider Trading:** Trading based on confidential company information.
- **Market Manipulation:** Creating artificial demand or supply to influence prices.
- **Front Running:** Brokers trading before executing client orders for their own profit.
- **Wash Trades:** Buying and selling the same stock to create fake trading volume.
- **Circular Trading:** Related parties executing trades among themselves to mislead the market.

Understanding these regulations is essential for traders and investors. Compliance with SEBI and exchange rules ensures a fair market for all participants. Being aware of the legal framework helps traders make informed decisions and navigate the market responsibly.

Conclusion

A strong legal and regulatory framework keeps the Indian derivatives market fair, transparent, and secure. SEBI, as the market watchdog, ensures that all participants follow the rules. Traders must understand key regulations to stay compliant and avoid penalties. Investor grievance redressal mechanisms protect traders' rights, while strict rules prevent fraudulent activities. By following these regulations, traders can operate safely and confidently in the market, ensuring a smooth and trustworthy trading environment for everyone.

Chapter 9: Taxation in Derivatives Trading

Arun- I want to know regarding Taxation in Derivatives Trading

Ravi- Yes, I will explain you , but it changes as per tax law. Regarding existing tax, I will share with you.

Taxation on Derivative Trading in India

Trading in derivatives, such as Futures and Options (F&O), is a popular activity in India. The taxation rules for F&O trading are different from regular stock investments. The Indian Income Tax Act classifies F&O transactions as **non-speculative business income** rather than capital gains. This means traders must report their profits and losses under the head **"Profits and Gains from Business or Profession"** while filing Income Tax Returns (ITR).

This document simplifies the taxation rules, including turnover calculation, tax audit requirements, advance tax payments, and loss treatment, with clear examples.

9.1. Tax Treatment of Derivatives

Business Income Classification

- **F&O trading is treated as business income**, not capital gains.
- Whether the trader is an individual, company, or partnership firm, the income is taxed as business income.
- Traders can deduct expenses such as brokerage, internet fees, and advisory charges.

Example: Ravi, an individual trader, made a profit of **₹3 lakh** from F&O trading and incurred expenses of **₹50,000** (brokerage, internet, and advisory fees). His taxable income from F&O trading will be **₹2.5 lakh (₹3 lakh - ₹50,000).**

9.2. Turnover Calculation

Turnover is an important metric to determine if a **tax audit** is required. It is calculated differently for futures and options:

- **For Futures:** Absolute sum of profits and losses across all trades.
- **For Options:** Sum of all premiums received and paid.

Futures Example:

Trader A's transactions in futures:

- Trade 1: Profit of **₹15,000**
- Trade 2: Loss of **₹12,500**

- Trade 3: Profit of **₹8,000**

Turnover = |₹15,000| + |₹12,500| + |₹8,000| = **₹35,500**

Options Example:

Trader B's transactions in options:

- Received premium: **₹9,000**
- Paid premium: **₹6,000**

Turnover = ₹9,000 + ₹6,000 = **₹15,000**

9.3. Tax Audit Requirements

A tax audit is **mandatory** if:

1. The total turnover exceeds **₹10 crore** (from FY 2021-22 onwards).
2. The trader declares income below **6% of turnover** under presumptive taxation.

Example: Trader C has a total turnover of **₹11 crore** from F&O trading. Since this is above the ₹10 crore limit, they must undergo a **mandatory tax audit**.

9.4. Presumptive Taxation (Section 44AD)

For small traders with a turnover of **up to ₹2 crore**, Section 44AD allows them to pay tax on a **presumed income of 6% of turnover**.

Example:

Trader D's turnover is **₹1.5 crore**. They opt for presumptive taxation.

Taxable Income = 6% of ₹1.5 crore = **₹9 lakh**

If their actual profit is **₹12 lakh**, they can choose to declare the higher amount and claim expenses.

9.5. Advance Tax Payments

Traders must pay advance tax if their total tax liability exceeds ₹10,000 in a financial year.

Advance Tax Schedule:

- **June 15** – 15% of total tax
- **September 15** – 45% of total tax
- **December 15** – 75% of total tax
- **March 15** – 100% of total tax

Example:

Trader E expects a total tax liability of **₹2 lakh**. They must pay:

- ₹30,000 by June 15 (15%)
- ₹60,000 by September 15 (additional 30%)
- ₹60,000 by December 15 (additional 30%)
- ₹50,000 by March 15 (remaining 25%)

9.6. Loss Treatment

Offsetting Losses

- **F&O losses can be set off** against other business income in the same financial year.

Carrying Forward Losses

- If losses cannot be adjusted, they can be carried forward for **8 years**.
- Losses can only be set off against **business profits** in future years.

Example: Trader F incurs an **F&O loss of ₹5 lakh** and earns a profit of **₹7 lakh** from another business. The loss can be adjusted against the profit, resulting in a net taxable business income of **₹2 lakh**.

9.7. ITR Forms for Filing

- **ITR-3:** For traders declaring **business income**.
- **ITR-4:** For those opting for **presumptive taxation** under Section 44AD.

9.8. Key Deductions

Under normal taxation, traders can deduct expenses such as:

- Brokerage charges
- Data subscriptions
- Internet costs
- Advisory fees
- Office rent

9.9. Securities Transaction Tax (STT)

STT applies to derivative trading as follows:

- **Futures:** 0.01% on the **sell-side**
- **Options:** 0.05% on **sell-side premium**

Example: Trader G sells an option contract with a premium of ₹10,000. STT = **0.05% of ₹10,000 = ₹5**

9.10. Potential Changes in Taxation

The Indian government is considering **classifying F&O income as speculative income**. If implemented, these changes may occur:

1. **TDS of 30%** on F&O transactions.
2. **No set-off of F&O losses** against other business income.
3. **Taxation similar to crypto trading or lottery winnings.**

These changes would significantly impact traders. It is advisable to stay updated with government policies and seek professional tax advice.

Conclusion

Understanding taxation in derivatives trading is very important for every trader. Proper knowledge of tax treatment, turnover calculation, audit rules, and advance tax can help avoid legal issues and penalties. Choosing the right ITR form and knowing how to treat losses can also reduce tax burdens. Additionally, being aware of deductions and STT ensures better financial planning. Since tax rules may change, traders must stay updated and consult experts to remain compliant and optimize their tax liabilities.

Chapter 10: Building a Winning Trader's Mindset - The Key to Long-Term Success

Why Do 90% of Option Traders Lose Money?

Arun: Ravi, SEBI reports that 90% of derivative traders lose money in the options market. Can you explain why this happens?

Ravi: Sure, Arun. The two primary reasons are **overtrading** and **lack of risk management**.

Arun: That sounds serious! What should a trader do to avoid these pitfalls?

Ravi: The key is to follow disciplined trading rules. Here are two essential rules that can have a significant positive impact on your trading results:

Rule 1: Limit the Number of Trades

- Never take more than **two trades per day**.
- If your first trade is profitable, **stop trading for the day**—don't let greed take over.

- If your first trade results in a loss, you may take **one more trade**, but not beyond that.

Rule 2: Risk Only 1% of Your Capital Per Trade

- Never risk more than **1% of your total trading capital** on a single trade.
- For example, if your trading capital is **₹2,00,000**, your maximum loss per trade should not exceed **₹2,000**.
- Always set a **stop-loss** and exit the position when the loss limit is reached.

By following these two rules, traders can develop discipline, avoid unnecessary losses, and maintain long-term success in the options market.

Understanding the Trader's Mindset

Now, let's dive deeper into the psychology of trading and how mastering your emotions can make all the difference...

Alright, so you've learned about derivatives, strategies, and market analysis. But guess what? All that knowledge is only *part* of the battle. The *real* secret to success in trading lies in your *mindset*. Think of your mind as the engine of a car; it needs to be tuned properly to win the race!

This chapter isn't about *what* to trade, but *how* to think. We'll cover key psychological principles that separate consistently profitable traders from those who constantly struggle.

10.1: Why Mindset Matters More Than You Think

Many new traders focus solely on finding the "perfect" strategy or the "hot" stock tip. They think that's all it takes to make money. But think about it, if trading was so easy, wouldn't everyone be rich?

The truth is, the market is unpredictable. Strategies that work today might fail tomorrow. That's where your mindset comes in. A strong mindset helps you:

Manage Emotions: Fear and greed can make you do crazy things! A good mindset keeps your emotions in check.

Stay Disciplined: Following your trading plan, even when it's tough, is crucial. Mindset helps you stick to the plan.

Learn from Mistakes: Everyone makes losing trades. A winning mindset helps you analyze your mistakes and improve.

Adapt to Change: The market is always changing. You need to be able to adjust your strategies and stay flexible.

10.2: Rule #1 - Master Your Emotions, Master Your Trades

This is the most important rule of all. Emotions like fear and greed are your *enemies* in the market.

Fear: Makes you sell too early, locking in a small profit or even a loss, because you're scared the market will crash.

Greed: Makes you hold on for too long, hoping for even more profit, even when it's time to exit. Then, the price falls, and you lose everything!

Practical Example: Imagine you bought a call option on Reliance, thinking the price will go up. It starts going up, and you are already in profit, but you are fearful that the stock will fall any moment and you will lose your profits, so you sell it quickly for a small profit and feel happy. Now, after you sell, the stock continues to go up much further. Here, fear didn't let you make the most out of the trade.

Solution:

Have a Trading Plan: Before you enter a trade, know your entry price, target price, and stop-loss. Stick to the plan, no matter what your emotions tell you.

Keep a Trading Journal: Write down why you made each trade, what your emotions were, and whether you followed your plan. See patterns in your emotional behavior and work on controlling them.

Take Breaks: Constantly watching price movements can stir up emotions. Walk away and clear your head.

10.3: Rule #2 - Detach from the Outcome

It's easy to get caught up in the results – the profits! But obsessing over profits leads to poor decisions. You might chase profits, take unnecessary risks, or panic when things don't go as planned.

Practical Example: Let's say you have a strategy that gives you a 60% win rate. But this week, you've had three losing trades in a row. You start doubting your strategy and make impulsive decisions to "win back" the money you lost. This is because you are too attached to the outcome and forgetting about the long-term.

Solution:

Focus on the Process: Focus on executing your trading plan consistently. Good trades, one at a time, will lead to profits in the long run.

Accept Losses: No strategy wins every time. Losses are part of the game. Don't let a few losses derail you.

Think Like an Operator: Your job is to execute the strategy, not to "own" the outcome.

10.4: Rule #3 - Respect Risk, Don't Fear It

Risk is inherent in trading. You can't eliminate it, but you can manage it. Fearing risk leads to hesitation and missed opportunities. Ignoring risk leads to disaster.

Practical Example: A new trader puts all his money into one stock because he heard it was a "sure thing." He's ignoring the risk of losing everything if that stock goes down. On the other hand, another trader is so afraid of losing money that she never makes a trade, missing out on potential profits.

Solution:

Understand Your Risk Tolerance: How much money are you willing to lose on a single trade?

Use Stop-Loss Orders: Set a price at which you will automatically exit a trade to limit your losses.

Diversify Your Portfolio: Don't put all your eggs in one basket. Spread your investments across different assets.

10.5: Rule #4 - The Market is Always Right

This is a tough one to swallow. Even if you've done your research and have a strong conviction, the market can prove you wrong. Arguing with the market is a losing battle.

Practical Example: You believe a stock is undervalued and buy it. But the price keeps falling. You keep buying more, convinced you're right, and the market is wrong. Eventually, the stock crashes, and you lose a lot of money.

Solution:

Be Flexible: Be willing to change your mind if the market is telling you something different.

Don't Get Emotionally Attached to Trades: It's just a trade, not a personal attack.

Use Stop-Loss Orders: If the market goes against you, exit the trade and move on.

10.6: Rule #5 - Patience Pays More Than Speed

Many new traders want to get rich quickly. They overtrade, taking every signal they see, hoping to hit a home run. But trading is not a sprint; it's a marathon.

Practical Example: A day trader makes dozens of trades every day, trying to capture every small price movement. He spends hours glued to the screen, stressed and exhausted. He ends up making small profits but also accumulating lots of small losses.

Solution:

Wait for High-Probability Setups: Don't force trades. Be patient and wait for the best opportunities.

Don't Overtrade: More trades don't equal more profit. Quality over quantity.

Focus on Long-Term Gains: Think about building wealth over time, not getting rich overnight.

10.7: Rule #6 - Stay Humble or Be Humbled

The market has a way of humbling even the most experienced traders. Overconfidence is a dangerous trap.

Practical Example: A trader has a few winning trades and starts to think he's a genius. He increases his position size, ignores his risk management rules, and makes reckless decisions. Inevitably, he loses a lot of money.

Solution:

Never Stop Learning: The market is always evolving. Keep learning and improving your skills.

Be Open to Feedback: Listen to other traders and be willing to learn from their experiences.

Acknowledge Your Mistakes: Everyone makes mistakes. Don't try to hide them. Learn from them.

10.8: The Journey of a Trader

Becoming a successful trader is a journey, not a destination. It requires constant learning, self-reflection, and discipline. The mindset principles we've discussed in this chapter are essential tools for navigating the challenges and achieving long-term success in the market. Remember, it's not just about the strategies; it's about *you*. By mastering your mind, you can master the market. Now go out there and trade with confidence and discipline!

Conclusion

A strong mindset is the foundation of long-term success in trading. Emotions, ego, and impatience can lead to losses, while discipline, risk management, and humility help traders grow. Accepting that the market is always right and focusing on the process instead of quick profits is key. Every trader's journey is full of ups and downs, but with the right mindset, learning never stops. Success comes to those who stay patient, humble, and committed to continuous improvement.

Summary and Conclusion

This book serves as a complete guide to understanding and mastering the world of equity derivatives in India. It starts with the fundamentals, explaining what derivatives are, their evolution, and their role in modern finance. The basics of stock market indices, which act as a market's pulse, are also covered to help traders interpret trends effectively.

The book then dives into the core instruments of derivatives trading—Forwards, Futures, and Options. It explains how these contracts work, their key features, and practical applications, making complex concepts easy to grasp. Various strategies such as hedging, speculation, arbitrage, and delta hedging are discussed to help traders make informed decisions.

To succeed in trading, understanding the market's functioning is crucial. The book explains how stocks qualify for derivatives trading, the impact of corporate actions, algorithmic trading, and the importance of analyzing futures and options data. It also sheds light on the behind-the-scenes operations, including clearing, settlement, and risk management, ensuring that traders are aware of what happens after they place a trade.

A crucial aspect of derivatives trading is compliance with regulations. The book outlines SEBI's role, key legal frameworks, investor protection measures, and prohibited activities to ensure traders operate within the rules. Taxation is another critical factor, and the book simplifies the tax treatment of derivatives, turnover calculation, tax audit requirements, and important deductions, helping traders stay tax-compliant.

Finally, the book emphasizes the significance of a winning trader's mindset. Trading success is not just about knowledge and strategies but also about emotional control, discipline, and patience. Key psychological rules, such as detaching from the outcome, respecting risk, and staying humble, are discussed to help traders sustain long-term success.

Final Thoughts

Trading in derivatives is a journey that requires continuous learning, discipline, and adaptability. Understanding the technical, regulatory, and psychological aspects of trading can set a strong foundation for success. While market movements are uncertain, a well-prepared trader, armed with the right knowledge and mindset, can navigate volatility with confidence.

The key takeaway from this book is that successful trading is not just about making money—it is about managing risk, maintaining discipline, and staying emotionally balanced. As markets evolve, so should traders. By applying the concepts covered in this book, traders can build a strong foundation for long-term success in derivatives trading.

May I ask you for a small favour?

Thank you for choosing to read this book. I know there are countless options out there, and I deeply appreciate that you picked mine. I hope it brought you value, offered some useful insights, and that you enjoyed the experience.

If you could spare just 30 more seconds, I have a small request. Would you consider leaving a review of the book?

For authors like me, who don't have a large following, reviews make a world of difference. They help others discover my work and encourage readers to take a chance on my books. Simply put, reviews are the lifeblood of any author's journey.

Your feedback doesn't have to be lengthy—just a few words sharing your thoughts would mean so much to me. It takes less than a minute, but it would tremendously help me reach more readers.

Thank you again for your support, and I'd love to hear your thoughts!